Living the RV Lifestyle

Practical Advice and Personal Tales from Life on the Road

Also by Donna M. Fisher-Jackson, M.A.

The Healing Path of the Romantic:
Type Four of the Enneagram Personality Type System

Clara & Irving: A Love Story of Past Lives

Living the RV Lifestyle

Practical Advice and Personal Tales from Life on the Road

DONNA FISHER-JACKSON

Wandering Way Printing Press

Cape Cod, Massachusetts

This book is written in the spirit of helping new or current Rvers learn more about camping and how to become Full-Time Rvers. We're not experts, and can't predict how our suggestions will affect your personal camping experience. We do hope that you'll enjoy the Full-time RV life as much as we do.

Copyright © 2017 Donna Fisher-Jackson

Cover and Book design, and Photographs by J. Alan Jackson

Cover photo of Donna and Jim Jackson was taken at the Wahweap RV & Campground on Lake Powell in Page, Arizona

Back Cover photo of Bighorn RV on the way to Panguitch, Utah

All rights reserved. No part of this book may be used or reproduced by any means, graphic, electronic, or mechanical including photocopying, recording, taping, or by any information storage retrieval system without the written permission of the author except in the case of brief quotations embodied in critical articles and reviews.

Books, articles, or websites quoted or cited in the text are covered under the usual fair allowances, and credit has been given to the authors and/or business owners.

ISBN-10: 1544785321
ISBN-13: 978-1544785325

For more information, visit www.DonnaFisherJackson.com

CONTENTS

	Dedication	i
	Acknowledgments	ii
	Preface	iv
	Introduction	vi
1	Is Full-time RVing for you?	1
2	Choosing the RV of your Dreams	4
3	Preparing for the Full-time RV journey	13
4	Transition Time: Leaving your Traditional Life behind for Living in an RV	42
5	RV Basics - Before you go	47
6	Staying Safe with your RV	51
7	Traveling with your Pets	56
8	Staying Connected on the Road	62
9	RV Camping Options	71
10	Working and Volunteering on the Road	93
11	Mishaps and Adventures of RV Life	101
12	National Park Tour	113
13	Hiking: Our Favorite Pastime	123
14	Pacific Coast Adventures	135
15	Exit Strategy	145
	About the Photographer	153

About the Author 155

Resource section 156

Special Note: To view all the pictures in this book in color, go to www.DonnaFisherJackson.com under Books by Donna.

DONNA FISHER-JACKSON

DEDICATION

For my parents, Donald and Doris Fisher, who instilled a love of travel in me and my sisters, Doreen Parker and Denise Fisher, and now, through their own children, Jennifer Parker Duffen and Jacob Donald Fisher, the journey continues.

ACKNOWLEDGMENTS

A book of any kind always takes so many more people than the author to make it a reality. First of all, I would have never been on this RV journey if it wasn't for my husband, Jim, who had a dream to travel around this great country, and visit national parks, and other places of natural beauty. I am grateful to him for convincing me to follow this RV dream which has turned out to be more incredible than I could have ever imagined. Thanks to Jim for his many gifts including all the photographs and book design, making this book a joint project. His love and support helped me to have the time and energy to write this book.

A big thank you also to my sister, Denise, who allowed us more than once to camp in her driveway, supporting us in our RV dream, and being the caretaker of our belongings as we traveled around the country. Someday, we hope to go RVing with my sisters, Denise and Doreen, and my nephew, Jacob, and my niece, Jennifer; sharing in the family's love of traveling.

Thanks also to my California friends who inspired me to write about my life on the road. Their support through Facebook, emails, and phone calls kept me going when I was miles away from my west coast "home." A special thanks to my friend, Barbara D'Amore, who helped select the perfect title for the book. Thanks to my friend, Gloria Gressman, who helped with cover ideas, and for her supportive friendship over the miles. Thanks to my friend, Sharon Gilmore, who always kept in touch with phone calls, cards, and gifts even when she had trouble tracking me down.

A special tribute to my dear friend, Chatham Forbes, Sr. who was one of my biggest fans who supported my earlier books, and my travels. He was an inspiration to me, teaching and taking people on trips for many years to historical sights, and places of amazing beauty around the world. His love of travel was contagious, and his ability to remember all the facts, and details of places was astonishing. I always told him that he should be the one writing books, but he was always busy living and loving life. He passed away in February, 2016 when I was on this RV journey. I miss his earthly presence, but I know he's still with me wherever I go.

Thanks to the other Full-time Rvers who offered their help, advice and support when Jim and I were just newbies on the road. I hope that we've also been able to help others who are just starting out on the RV journey. At least, that's what I hope this book will do for others who have a dream of the RV lifestyle.

PREFACE

When I tell people that Jim and I are on a Full-time RV journey, I often see a longing in their eyes. Some gaze dreamingly, and others speak openly about how they'd love to have the freedom to travel around the country. Throughout our travels, we've heard these comments from people: "I've always wanted to do that;" "That's the way to see the country;" "That would be my favorite way to travel;" and the all-time favorite, "That's always been my dream."

In the midst of my journey around the country, I discovered John Steinbeck's book, *Travels with Charley: In Search of America* about his own trip around the United States. In his late 50's, Steinbeck decided he wanted to take a trip around the country to see America up close – the country that he wrote about so often in his novels. It was 1960, and it had been twenty-five years since he had explored what the country was all about – the different regions, climates, terrains, and the people. He wanted to ride along the country roads, and avoid the highways as much as possible. In order to not have people recognize him by his name, Steinbeck decided to not stay in motels, but to travel the back roads in a camper. So he had a custom camper built on the back of a brand-new truck – his own version of the truck camper. He outfitted it with all the basics and more – a double bed, a four burner stove, a heater, refrigerator, a chemical toilet, and lots of storage. The storage cabinets overflowed with all the items he thought he might need including tools, emergency food, writing supplies, reference books, and all those books that he meant to read. Like most people on their first RV trip, he overloaded the camper, taxing his truck.

One of the themes that Steinbeck did share was the longing that many people expressed when they spied his truck camper. Steinbeck wrote how he saw in their eyes this burning desire to go, to get away, to be free, and to not necessarily move towards something but away from something. He wrote that he saw this look, and heard this yearning in every state that he visited. I smiled as I read his words, because I've had the same experience before I left on this journey, and while I've been traveling. I wonder what Steinbeck would think now if he knew that people still have that same longing all these years later. Some human experiences remain the same over the years.

As I've reflected on this universal longing, I think it's that natural desire to escape the world of work and responsibilities. We all have moments when we dream of a life with less obligations weighing us down. Many people daydream about retirement as a time when they will finally be free to travel and do as they please.

That's when it came to me. I am not just living my RV dream, but I am living this dream for many others. Many people aren't able to travel like this because they still have family and work obligations. They have children to take care of, and homes and businesses. They still have parents that need their time and attention. Being in a unique position - without children, without parents anymore, without a home, and without full-time jobs - my husband, Jim, and I are free to travel, and create work opportunities along the way. And that's how we came to be "Living the RV Lifestyle" which I now want to share with others through this book.

Donna Fisher-Jackson

INTRODUCTION

Since 2014, we've been Full-time Rvers. My husband, Jim, and I, and our traveling cat, Zeus, have made two big circles around the United States along with some crisscrossing. We've traveled over 36,900 miles, crossed 44 state lines, visited 36 national parks, and stayed in 73 RV parks, 3 Wal-Marts, One casino, and a family driveway.

View of Yosemite Valley from the Tunnel View overlook in Yosemite National Park in California. The view includes El Capitan, Half Dome, Sentinel Rock, Cathedral Rocks and Bridalveil Fall.

We arrived at the Full-time RV lifestyle after significant changes in our lives which I write about in the coming chapters. We hadn't been dreaming of the RV life, and yet, over a short amount of time, it became the next step for us. These three years have been incredible with the amount of experiences that we've had, from the city to the country, from the Northeast to the Southeast, and from the Southwest to the Northwest, and everywhere in between. We've covered a lot of ground, and seen some of the most amazing sights this country has to offer. Full-time RVing is definitely a trip of a lifetime, but it's more than a camping trip. It's a lifestyle choice that will change your life in ways that are hard to imagine at the beginning of the journey. If you can be flexible and willing to try new things, you will get the most out of this RV adventure.

This book can assist you with your own RV Dreams whether it's Full-time, Part-time or Anytime. I've included practical advice on how to explore if this RV dream is really what you are seeking. There are ways to test the water without committing thousands of dollars in the beginning. Many people rent an RV for a summer vacation, and others will borrow a friend's rig to try it out for a trip. Both are excellent ways to check out the experience.

If you've been camping for years on week-ends and vacations, then you're even closer to the Full-time RVing experience. Perhaps, take a longer trip and go away for a month, and see how you enjoy it. If you're still talking to your partner after that trip, then you're ready for a longer adventure. Some RVers who aren't quite ready to take the Full-time plunge will also rent out their home before selling it. I've met people on the road who rented their home out for a year, and planned on returning to their home once the lease ended. At that point, I am sure they had a better idea if Full-time RVing was for them.

I've also included sprinkled throughout the book, my personal RVing adventures with Jim, and our cat, Zeus. I hope the stories will give you some idea of what it's really like living on the road, along with ideas of what to see and do in your own travels around the country. Now, it's time to explore the world of RVing.

Chapter One

Is Full-time RVing for you?

What is Full-time RVing? It is a lifestyle choice – the choice to sell your traditional home or give up renting an apartment/condo to live in a Recreational Vehicle (RV) that you can move around to different locations, and work and live in wherever you may be at the time. The RV is your only home. (There are also people who live in their RV for six to nine months, and they are known as extended timers or part-time Full-Timers because they also own another home.)

If you love to travel, meet people from different areas of the country and even the world, enjoy being out in nature, and want a simpler life with more freedom, then Full-Time RVing could be the lifestyle choice that you're seeking. Without a traditional home, your cost of living is a lot lower, but it does still take some money especially in the beginning if you need to buy your RV, and possibly a truck to tow it.

In my travels around the country, I've seen solo RVers out here on the road along with some young families who are home schooling their children, and giving them the educational experience of a lifetime. But many of the Full-time RVers are couples. If you want to test the strength and love of your relationship, then become a Full-time RVer. Not only are you living in a smaller space, but you're also getting to spend more time with your partner than you've probably ever spent with them in your whole life together.

Some couples do a lot together, and other couples enjoy having more separate activities than together activities. Being a counselor, I have seen many different couple relationships, and it's really what works for you. If you enjoy spending a lot of time with your partner, and have many shared interests, then you will probably do well in the Full-time RVing lifestyle. Even with that said, there are going to be times when you both need some space and time away from each other. Some couples on the road handle those needs by participating in different activities at the campground, and others by having jobs on the road whether it's their own business, or working at a campground. The time apart seems to do wonders for most people. It comes down to finding that balance between spending time together, and time doing your own thing. It is certainly something to think about before you choose the Full-time RVing lifestyle.

If you're the type of person who likes to have your own space – a man cave, or a room of your own – it can be a big adjustment. A large RV is still only about 400 square feet with usually one large living room/kitchen/dining area, a bathroom, and a bedroom – not a lot of personal space. I am definitely the kind of person who enjoys having a room of her own, and time alone. Going for a walk around the campground by myself didn't always meet those needs. Eventually, I expressed my needs on this subject with my husband, and it did improve. Especially, when he began to have workamping jobs which were from 20 to 40 hours a week, then, I had some time alone to write, work at my own counseling business, and pursue my own interests. That improved my sense of well-being and my adjustment to living in a smaller space. (Workamping is a phrase coined by *Workamper News* at www.workamper.com with the official definition: "Workampers are adventuresome individuals and couples who have chosen a wonderful lifestyle that combines any kind of part-time or full-time work with RV camping." For more details on workamping, refer to Chapter 10 in this book.)

With that said, I've had some of the most remarkable experiences of my life on this RV journey, and also have had to stretch way out of my comfort zone. It's been liberating, eye-opening, challenging, heart-stopping and certainly never boring. If you're ready to let go of your traditional life, and take a chance on a fresh start, living with a lot less material possessions, but so much more freedom, then you're ready to be a Full-time RVer. It's time to make your dream a reality.

Donna and Jim in Sedona, Arizona

Chapter Two

Choosing the RV of your Dreams

An RV is built for travel. They are designed to move around, a lot. As one RV dealer told us, the quality RVs are built to withstand an earthquake because that's how it feels to your RV when it is being driven on the highway. Every time you take it out on the road, it's going through its own personal earthquake. If you're going to choose to be a Full-time RVer, you should choose a quality RV. The market is flooded right now with RV choices, but if this is going to be your full-time home, you want to know that it's going to last longer than a season. If you are a Part-timer, camping only once and a while, and maybe a week here or there, then a tow-behind Travel Trailer could be fine, or a less expensive Class A mobile home or Class B, a camping van, or even a Truck Camper. But if you're going Full-time, then you need to research your options.

There are companies that sell RV reports that rate and review a wide variety of RVs. The company that we used was, JR Consumer Resources Inc. through www.RVReviews.net. If you find an RV that you really like, then it's wise to purchase the review from a company like JR Consumer Resources, Inc., and get some inside information as well as check on-line for other reviews. You will not be sorry if you do some of the checking beforehand. In the less expensive RVs, a lot can go wrong, and it does. At campgrounds around the country, I see mobile RV repair trucks showing up almost every week, fixing someone's RV. There may be minor problems like a broken lock, but sometimes, there are major issues like a slide-out that won't go back in, or a heater that needs repair. Keeping up with RV maintenance is definitely key to a "Happy Camper."

Before I go any further, I want to address the topic of Tiny Homes. Tiny Home shows are very popular on TV. Many people consider buying these smaller versions of a real home on wheels to take around the country. After all my years on the road, I've only seen one Tiny Home being towed behind a truck. It was in a South Dakota campground. This little wooden house with a back porch pulled in late one night, and left early the next morning so I never got to talk to the owner of this quaint home. I imagined that it was headed to a plot of land where it is still living today. Tiny homes are a great idea for down-sizing and living in a smaller space, but realistically, they are not built for travel. With all the wear and tear that comes from highway travel, I don't think the Tiny Home would last more than several months on the road, if that. If you want to travel with your home around the country, the RV is the best choice for you.

In the world of RVs, there are three main types of RVs which include: **Motor Homes** (including those Fancy Buses), **Trailers** (towed behind a truck), and **Truck Campers** (They go on the back of a pick-up truck.)

Under **Motor Homes**, there are different classes including **Class A** – the largest of the group with the most amenities, and best suited for Full-time living; **Class B** – a smaller size motor home which looks more like a van. They have the basics, but they seem too small for the Full-time lifestyle; **Class C** – These motor homes can be as long as a Class A, but what gives them a different look is the front which looks like the cab of a truck with a section above which usually holds a bed. Some are roomy, but they may not be as suited for towing a vehicle which means you have to take your home with you wherever you go. Most Full-timers don't want to have to move their home every time they want to go sight-seeing, or to the store. It's nice to tow an extra vehicle to drive.

In the **Trailer** category, there are two types suitable for Full-time living: the Travel Trailer and the Fifth Wheel. The **Travel Trailer** is a large trailer towed completely behind the tow vehicle. They are hitched to the back of the tow vehicle which can be anything that has enough power to pull the trailer. They are also usually less expensive. The **Fifth Wheel** is a trailer that has a gooseneck or king pin front section that extends over the bed of the pick-up truck that will be towing it. The hitch is located in the center of the truck bed, so fifth wheels can only be towed by a pick-up or flatbed truck. With the hitch inside the truck as opposed to on the bumper, it gives the Fifth Wheel more stability and less chance of jack-knifing and fish-tailing. The trucks do need to be medium duty or even heavy duty with dual wheels depending on the size of the trailer. Matching your Fifth Wheel with the right truck that can pull its weight when loaded is key. A great website for help with matching a truck with a Fifth Wheel is www.fifthwheelst.com.

There is also a specialized travel trailer called a **Toy Hauler** which has a back compartment with a large door that turns into a ramp. They are great for storing motorcycles, all-terrain vehicles (ATVs), and possibly a small car. Some of the Toy Haulers even have bunk beds that fold down in the back compartment, perfect for a traveling family.

Most Full-time RVers tend to choose from these two options more than any other: the **Class A Mobile Home**, and the **Fifth Wheel**. I have read one Full-time RVing book where the couple sold everything to live in a truck camper and made it work, but I think it only works if you enjoy being really close to your partner, and don't have a lot of stuff or pets. This couple also turned their shower into a closet, so they had to use campground bathrooms wherever they went which is another option. Truthfully, I think the truck camper is too small for most couples who are Full-timing.

Both the Class A Mobile Home and Fifth Wheel seem to be the most appealing to Full-Timers because of the living space. I've never heard a Full-timer complain that their RV is too big. They may not enjoy towing or driving the big rig every day especially in city areas, but they do love the extra space. It certainly comes in handy when you're living with a spouse, or even a couple of children and not to mention, the pets. The bigger RV becomes the better solution. The two choices seem to be a matter of preference. Personally, I have owned a Fifth Wheel, and not a Class A Mobile Home, but I have talked to Full-timers with the Class A Mobile Home. These are some of the advantages and disadvantages.

Class A Mobile Home – Advantages:

Easier to drive. Self-contained. A passenger can do other activities like sit at a kitchen table with their seat belt on. Easier when you stop at a rest area, and can access your bathroom right away. Can tow a car/boat. Don't have to buy a second vehicle even, or a large truck. They have more storage space underneath. When you arrive in inclement weather, you can stay in the mobile home until ready to hook up the utilities. Many have self-leveling jacks so no need for blocks.

Disadvantages: Motorhomes can be more expensive even when you compare the cost of a truck and a trailer. Cost of motor home maintenance is higher, especially if you have two engines to maintain including the vehicle you're towing. Your RV home can also end up in the garage, and then you may need to find alternate lodging which can be expensive. Have to take the whole vehicle to the gas station or to fill up propane. Can't have a ceiling fan because of the restrictions in ceiling heights. Have less living space with car seats and the front engine. Mobile home insurance is higher than for a Fifth Wheel. They also depreciate faster because of the engine.

Fifth Wheel Trailer – Advantages:

Many Full-timers believe the Fifth Wheel feels the most like a home without the driving seats in the way. You only have one engine, the truck engine to worry about. If your truck has to get some work done in the garage, then you can still stay in your Fifth Wheel home. The ceiling in the living room area is higher so you can have a ceiling fan. Fifth Wheels are usually less expensive.

Disadvantages: You do need to buy a heavy duty truck that can tow a trailer that's anywhere from 10,000 – 18,000 pounds. When you arrive at a campground, you do have to get out to set it up even if it has self-leveling jacks. You can't ride in your camper while you're towing it. Once you un-hitch from the RV, the truck can be cumbersome to drive around as your only vehicle. Hitching/unhitching, towing and backing up can be challenging until you get it down. If you have to finance the purchase, the tow vehicle (truck) loan cannot be spread out like an RV loan so your monthly payments could be higher on a trailer/tow vehicle combination than on a motorhome.

For Full-time RVing, it comes down to a personal preference. I have met Full-timers who have tried both types, and have enjoyed the variety. As far as whether to buy new or used, that's also a matter of preference. Some people only want new which is great, but like a car, the value of the RV goes down immediately when you drive it off the lot. You also have to work out some of the issues of a new RV that haven't been tested yet by anyone. The cost is also a big factor. There are lots of deals out there on used RVs, but again, you want to do your research, and check them out thoroughly before purchasing a used one. You may also want to buy a less expensive RV to see if the Full-time RV lifestyle is for you, then you haven't invested a lot of money, and you can always upgrade later. Take your time and consider your options. Visit some RV Dealer lots, and go to some RV shows but, don't buy one at show without some consideration. In the excitement of being at a show, you may make the wrong decision. With your research, you'll start to get a better idea of what type of RV you would like best.

You may also want to rent an RV before you buy, just to get a feel for the lifestyle especially if you've never RVed in the past. It's not always easy to find a rental for the exact motor home that you're considering, but try to find one that duplicates the experience. When you're in the RV, imagine yourself living in it full-time with your partner, family and pets. Try out all the systems on board. Drive it around in different areas on back roads, and highways. My husband and I couldn't find a reasonable rental for a week so we didn't try one out, but in hindsight, even borrowing a friend's RV might have been helpful. After several months of research, we decided to take the plunge into the RV lifestyle with no previous RV vacationing experience, and it all worked out.

Finding our Dream RV

This is the short version of how Jim and I found the RV of our dreams. After selling our home in California, and before we headed back to Massachusetts to settle our family estates, my husband researched RVs as a possible Full-time home for the future. He decided on the Fifth Wheel Trailers as opposed to Class A Motor Homes because they felt more like homes. After researching all the quality RVs out there, Jim came up with a list of the top brands for Fifth Wheels including New Horizons, DRV Luxury Suites and NuWa/Kansas RV Center.

After getting in touch with the top company on his list, New Horizons, we planned on stopping at their Kansas headquarters to have a tour of their manufacturing plant, and to look at a couple of used New Horizons which were now being sold by the former owners. All the RVs built by New Horizons are custom designed and built for the owners. New Horizons does fill a specialized niche in the RV industry, but it's an expensive option for most people. We thought we'd check out these used RVs to see if any appealed to us. After an extensive tour, we found a used Fifth Wheel that we liked. It was higher than what we wanted to pay at $99,900. With some negotiation, Jim thought they might lower the price.

Once we arrived on the east coast, we became busy with the family estates, and decided to wait on the purchase. Jim continued to call the New Horizons salesperson, and check their website, but still no change in price. After we settled the estates, about three months later, Jim was still negotiating with New Horizons, but for some reason, they wouldn't budge on the price. To clear our heads, we decided to go for a walk on the Cape Cod Canal.

When Jim and I strolled by the Bourne Scenic RV Park, it was mid-September so there weren't a lot of RVs in the park. Children and college students had gone back to school, and now the retirees could head out on the road for some sightseeing without the crowds. Cape Cod is still a busy place in the fall. But during the week, you can walk beaches all by yourself, and still savor seafood by the ocean without the summer crowds.

So there we were taking a more serious look at RVs especially the Fifth Wheel style because it felt most like a home. Jim was still focused on the New Horizons RV, but that was way back in Kansas, a long drive from Cape Cod. As we walked along gravel paths through the park, I spied a Bighorn RV with a For Sale sign. No one seemed to be around, but the RV had a prime spot, right on the canal with a view of the sailboats and ships going by. I snapped pictures, and copied the details down while Jim kept walking. I mentioned that it could be worth a call because they were also selling the truck which was something we would have to buy even if we bought the New Horizons RV.

Jim ordered up the RV report from www.RVReviews.net and the 2011 39 foot Bighorn Fifth Wheel RV by Heartland received a positive rating. It also was a plus that the current owners had previously owned a 2009 model, and enjoyed it so much that they bought a 2011 when they wanted some extra features.

After a couple of phone calls, and two viewings, the Bighorn RV became our new home which also included the 2008 GMC Sierra 3500 HD truck with dual wheels. The current owners were also meticulous in their care of this RV and the truck, and included in the sale lots of the RV goodies that you need on the road. Retiring from RVing, they still had a home, and had only used the RV for winter trips to Florida, and summer trips locally. The owners also gave us their detailed check-lists for opening and closing the RV, and lots of tips for traveling with the RV.

The Bighorn RV also included other features that a friend had mentioned as being key: An electric fireplace which has come in handy on our more cooler camping experiences; a front hall closet with washer/dryer hookups, but we've chosen to use it as a closet, and to store our pet supplies; and lastly, having the kitchen table on the side with the door so you can overlook your own camp site instead of your neighbor's, a key feature in those extra small campgrounds.

The whole experience of buying the Bighorn RV, and the GMC Sierra truck turned out to be a case of being at the right place at the right time. So that would also be part of my advice. Look locally, don't get fixated on one RV, and be open to other possibilities including used models. Do your homework, and research, and you'll be ready when your RV shows up.

Chapter 3

Preparing for the Full-time RV journey

You're getting close to choosing your Dream RV. Now, it's time to prepare for the Full-Time life. For most people, there's a timing to the beginning of your new life on the road. Some have to give notice at their jobs. For others, it's the ending of their career, and moving into retirement. Whatever the situation, the main tasks are **Organizing your Finances, Clearing the Clutter, Selling Your House, Choosing your Home Base** (Domicile), and **Moving into your New RV Home** and **What to Pack for Life on the Road.**

Some people financially need to sell their primary home to fund this Full-time RVing adventure. Some keep a small cabin or vacation home, and that gives them a place to go back to as well as a home base for tax purposes. If you are able to eliminate all debt, you will feel a lot freer to live this lifestyle. I know that can be a big undertaking, but for most people, a home is their largest debt item along with the costs of living in a traditional home. Without that mortgage payment and the cost of living in that home, you will have more disposable income for your RV lifestyle.

What led to Our RV Journey

In our lives, the RV Dream presented itself when all of our parents had passed away. Over a period of three years, we lost three of our parents, and my husband's job situation changed. It was time for a big lifestyle change. In January, 2014, it became clear to me that we needed to sell our California home, and travel back east to take care of our parents' estates. After a great deal of thinking and planning, my husband and I prepared to begin the process.

Once the decision was made to get the home ready to sell, the other pieces fell into place. In March, we listed our home for sale just as my husband prepared to let his boss know of his intentions to leave the company. But before he could hand in his resignation that week, his company made a decision to close their Grass Valley, CA office, and move their headquarters to Texas. The synchronicity of the two events didn't escape me, and it just confirmed that we were on the right path of selling our home, and leaving California behind. Since we really didn't want to live in Texas, he made the decision to leave the company for good.

Our California home took six weeks to sell, giving us time to sort through everything, and prepare to move. After a couple of garage sales along with a lot of sales through craigslist, and donating/gifting the rest of the items, we ended up with enough items to fit into one of those PODS, a storage container that is dropped off in your driveway www.pods.com. You fill the container, and then call them to pick it up. The PODS company will then deliver the container with your stored items wherever you're moving, and if it's not going directly to a place right away, then they will store it for you. It turned out to be the best possible solution for us. We didn't have to rent a moving truck on our own to drive cross-country especially since we weren't moving into a permanent home. We needed to store the items for future use. When we were ready, we called them up, and they delivered the POD to my parents' former home, giving us time to unpack, and store the items.

From January through September, we became experts at cleaning out homes, preparing them to sell, and then moving on. In a sense, the nine months gave us the opportunity to birth our new RV lifestyle.

Organizing your Finances

Before you make that big commitment to the Full-time RV lifestyle, take a serious look at your finances, and what you've been spending your money on, and what you plan on letting go of for this big life change. Being as debt-free as possible is the best way to begin this journey. If you have credit cards, then pay them off every month, or as some Full-timers suggest only use the credit cards for emergencies, and pay with your debit card or cash for all your expenses. These can be big changes to the way you've been living your life, but it will free you up to live the RV dream.

Funding our RV Dream

In our situation, selling our home, and inheriting money from our parents' estates, allowed us to make this big lifestyle change. After that, we didn't have any debt other than credit cards that we paid off every month. Since we were in our 50's, we didn't have a social security check to depend on, or even a pension check. We needed to rely on our savings to start, and then later, my husband began his workamping career which gave us free rent at campgrounds, and usually included all the utilities as well as some extra income. I also continued to do my counseling work on the road, and receive some royalties from book sales.

At first, we didn't have a good idea of how much this RV lifestyle would cost. It was hard to come up with a budget, but after three months, on the road, it became clearer. In the first year, we were moving around a lot, every week or two so our monthly expenses were higher especially with campground fees and diesel fuel for the truck.

The second year, we stayed in campgrounds longer, and received a discount for a month or longer. The workamping jobs also cut our monthly expenses in half, but, we did stay and work in one place for four months at a time. In the third year, we've saved a lot with workamping jobs, and did some "Moochdocking" in my sister's driveway.

Depending on your personal financial situation, you may have enough fixed income to fund your time on the road, and not need to pick up workamping jobs for free rent. You may also be interested in volunteer opportunities at national and state parks which can be less demanding, and less restrictive on your time, and yet, often give you free rent at campgrounds while you're volunteering there.

In the beginning, it can be hard to know what your budget will be. A great RVing website which includes sample budgets is www.RV-Dreams.com managed by Howard and Lynda Payne who've been RVing since 2005, beginning their journey when they were only 41 years old. They've included budgets from the beginning of their Full-time adventure to now that will give you a good idea of how much you might need on the road. They also organize RV rallies where they instruct people on the Full-time RV lifestyle from newbies who may or may not even have their RV yet to Full-timers who want to learn some new skills, and meet others who are living on the road like them. It's a great way to receive a wealth of knowledge before you take the plunge.

Clearing the Clutter

Before you decide to sell your home, clearing the clutter earlier than later can save you a lot of hassle when it comes time for the big move. Because we had made a big cross-country move in the past along with a couple of other moves, we had some experience with letting go of material possessions. If you haven't moved in years, the clearing of the clutter could take longer. It's a very emotional process, going through all your belongings. Being a counselor, I thought I was prepared for the emotional aspects of the letting go, but after going through the letting go of my own home, and all of our parents' homes at the same time, I did go through a lot of grieving. In Chapter 4, I write more about the transition of leaving your house behind along with a community of family and friends. It's a big change on many levels. So there still may be some personal items that you want to keep for sentimental reasons, and that's where you'll need to look into your storage options whether it's a professional storage facility or at a relative's home.

Our Big Down-sizing

Before leaving California, we looked into the rents on storage units in that state, and the costs quickly woke us up to the fact that we really didn't want to be paying for a storage unit that costs as much as a studio apartment. Since we didn't know how long our items might be in storage, we knew that it could easily become a huge expense over the years. That's when we decided to really do some serious letting go of the material items in our home, keeping only the essential and sentimental items – the ones that couldn't be replaced.

We also came up with our own storage option - to build a storage shed from a kit on my family's property, and store what belongings we had left in it. When we do return someday and empty it, then the storage shed will now belong to my sister who bought my parents' home. As a thank you for the use of the land, Jim even hooked up security cameras to keep an eye on the shed, and the driveway which now belong to my sister as well. It's been very generous of my sister to allow us to leave a storage shed on her property.

In the letting go process, my husband became an expert at scanning documents and photographs so we eliminated a huge amount of files along with photo albums. He would scan the best pictures from the albums, and then throw away the whole album. Now, all of our photos are on the computer, and backed up on two back-up drives. The process also involved shredding hundreds of documents which luckily our great recycling company in California was happy to take off our hands. We did burn out one shredder in the process, but we have another smaller one on board the RV so we still continue to lighten our load along the way.

In 2014, craigslist was one of our best tools for selling items. We had buyers come to the home for larger items, and met the buyers in public places for smaller items. We had no suspicious incidents to report, but we did live in a more rural area in California. In a city, I would probably suggest meeting in public places, and bringing along a friend. The newer electronic items were sold on Amazon, and this worked well though you do have to be able to ship the items. We also had a couple of neighborhood garage sales which also moved a lot of items out our door. Then, we donated and gifted the rest of the items left even having Habitat for Humanity's Restore, and Salvation Army come to the house to pick up furniture, a refrigerator and other large items near the end of our time in the house.

When we left California, we also downsized to one car which we have continued to keep, storing it at a relative's home the first year when we moved around the country so often. In the second year, I drove the car all around the country, following Jim who drove the truck towing the Fifth Wheel. It's been great to have a second vehicle on the road, and gives the truck a break when we stay in one place for a few months. We still drive the truck every couple of weeks to keep the engine in top shape for the next move.

After selling, donating, gifting, storing and throwing away stuff, we whittled our belongings down to what we really wanted to bring with us on the RV journey. The big factor for your RV is the weight. You don't want to overload your RV, and make it unsafe to drive on the road. Each RV has weight limits as well as the towing capacities of trucks for the Travel Trailers and Fifth Wheels. Make sure you know those limits before you start loading up the RV. A great informative website on weight limits and towing capacities of vehicles for the Fifth Wheels is www.fifthwheelst.com . Three of the Escapees campgrounds in Congress, Arizona; Bushnell, Florida; and Livingston, Texas; can assist you with weighing your RV to make sure you have a good weight for the road. Some of the RV rallies also have scales to have your RV properly weighed. It's very important to have the weight checked because if you're in an accident, and your rig is overweight then the accident can be considered your fault.

We thought we were packing light. But in Florida on our first trip, we got weighed at the Escapees campground in January and the RV had to go on a serious diet. We weighed the RV again at the Escapees campground in Texas in February, and received an even more accurate weight which led us to ship back dishes, and other heavy items to my sister's home. We chose lighter dishes for the RV, and kept only essential cooking equipment. My husband also sent back some of his tools, and we even left the portable generator behind after our first year because we hadn't used it once. (If you're into boondocking which is camping on public land with no utilities, kind of like living off the grid, then you may need a generator. We only boondocked in a Wal-Mart parking lot, and have yet to try camping on public lands.) After our first trip around the country, we unloaded more stuff from the RV into our storage unit, and are now traveling a lot lighter on the road.

Selling your House

Deciding what to do with your current house is probably the biggest decision you'll make before buying your RV, and beginning your Full-time life on the road. Some people we met did keep their house, and rented it out. If you own your house with no mortgage, then this could be an alternative for you. If you have family or friends who want to rent the home furnished, or if you're willing to put your belongings in storage, and utilize a property manager's services to handle the rental, then it could work. Some people might even hire a house-sitter to keep an eye on their home while they're away traveling. These are all good options if you want to try out the Full-time RV lifestyle before committing 100 % to the lifestyle. You can be a part-time Full-timer, and that works well for some people which is going away for the winter and/or the summer months, and returning to their home base for the rest of the year.

It can be hard to let go of your traditional house. You may want to have a home to go back to. These are all good reasons to keep the house, but if you really want a life with freedom from belongings, then you'll need to let go of the house at some point. The selling of the house also greatly simplifies your life which is one of the appealing qualities of the RV lifestyle.

The Decision to Sell Our Home

My husband and I considered all these options. We talked to a friend who was a property manager who handled rental properties. After hearing all about the service fees, and even extra house insurance that we might need to have a rental, it didn't sound like a money-making proposition for us. We still had a mortgage on the house, and it didn't add up to rent the property. It wasn't an easy decision, but in hindsight, it was the best decision for us. We loved living in the Gold Country of California, but it was becoming more expensive to maintain our lifestyle in that state. Once we decided to sell the house, then it really freed us up to begin our new life.

Our situation was a little different because we had family estates to handle before we could head out on the open highway. We sold our own house before buying the RV, and for most people, it usually works out better that way especially if you still have a mortgage on your house. Then, you'll either have the cash on hand to buy the RV when it shows up, or you'll be able to finance it without having to worry about paying a mortgage on your house as well.

Our California home took six weeks to sell which seemed long at the time, but in hindsight, it gave us enough time to finish jobs, clear clutter, pack and ship the POD, and prepare to drive cross-country with our car. It also gave us time for all those good-byes with friends who had become like family over the years. As a counselor, it's always been important to me to have enough time for those endings with people, places and even things like your house.

If your house takes longer to sell, then you may end up buying the RV first. That may also work out if you're able to park it in your current driveway, or at a relative's home. That wasn't possible at our California house with a steep driveway, but at my parents' former house, it's a nice, flat driveway with plenty of room to park the RV. Once we settled our family estates, we parked in the driveway at the home my sister was buying. She was still in the middle of selling her home, so it turned out to be the best arrangement for all of us. We kept an eye on her new home to be, and were able to adjust to living in our new RV home in the driveway.

My husband moved in right away, and spent most of his time in the RV while I stayed in my parents' home some of the daytime, and made dinner there, and then slept in the RV at night. We each got to have time alone, and also time together, getting used to living in the smaller space. It also gave us time to get used to all the systems of the RV, and begin moving our belongings into the space as well. My husband also set up an electric plug at the home for our RV, and a connection into the town sewer which was for emptying the tanks of the RV. That way, when we came back to visit, we'd be able to do some more "Moochdocking" in my sister's driveway which we have done.

I would highly recommend trying out the RV this way in a stationary place so you can get more familiar with your new home, and how everything works. You may even want to practice driving it around town, and parking it back in the space which does take some practice. Some Full-timers also took driving lessons at this point, or made a visit to a RV rally, their first stop to learn more about the RV life as well as meeting up with other Full-timers who are usually only happy to help out the newbies on the road.

The timing of selling your home can be tricky. If it doesn't sell quickly, you may want to consider selling it furnished. We ended up selling some of our parents' homes furnished, and it allowed us to leave behind a lot of furniture that we really didn't need for our new lifestyle. It also saved some time in having to find buyers and/or places to donate all the belongings. If it gets down to the wire, and you're ready for your RV life to begin, then you may have to rent out your home, or have a house-sitter keep an eye on your property. Somehow, the timing seems to work for most people. I usually have faith that the right buyer for the house will show up when the time is right, just like the right RV will show up.

The whole Full-time RV lifestyle does take a leap of faith. In the beginning, I remember telling some people about what we had just done, and they perceived us as adventurous. Perhaps, they meant crazy, but were too polite to tell me that. Others thought I must be a gypsy, but somehow, my gypsy side had only shown up in my alternative counseling business – until now. Some of your family and friends won't understand or even support you in this lifestyle choice, but it's your chance to follow a dream that you may have had for a very, long time.

Choosing your Home Base

Once you decide to become a Full-time RVer, then you have to decide where you would like your home base to be for such purposes as receiving U.S. mail, your driver's license, registering your vehicles, paying taxes, purchasing health care, where you're registered to vote, where your will is drawn up, etc.

When you no longer have a permanent traditional home, then you need to choose a state for your legal domicile which is different from residency. You can be a resident in more than one state, but you can only have one legal domicile. In that one state, you have to establish contacts through such items as getting a mailing address, a driver's license, etc. The more contacts that you make in one state, then the state is more accepting that it really is your domicile. If you try to have your driver's license and vehicle registration in another state, then that state could claim you as a citizen of their state, and require you to pay their state property taxes and income taxes as well. Since you are simplifying your life, it's probably wise to pick one state, and have all your "contacts" there so it's clear that this is your legal domicile.

Many people decide to stick with their current home state out of convenience. Perhaps, you still have family there who can send you your mail, and you already have your driver's license there, and your vehicles registered there. But if you're interested in moving to a less expensive state with no income taxes, and lower property taxes and insurance rates, then you may want to shop around for your legal domicile.

State Income Tax can be one of the key deciding factors. The states with no state income taxes include: Alaska, Florida, Nevada, South Dakota, Texas, Washington state, and Wyoming. (New Hampshire and Tennessee also do not have a state income tax on salaries and wages, but they do have an interest and dividends tax which affects many retirees.)

Many Full-Timers find Florida, South Dakota and Texas to be the easiest states to choose as your domicile for the no state income tax rule. You may still want to compare the states because insurance premiums and property taxes, along with driver's license fees and vehicle registrations can vary a lot to see what the best deal is for you.

Personal property taxes vary from state to state, and some can charge a lot for your RV, and vehicles. **Vehicle registration fees** also vary, and are worth checking out especially if there are any requirements on regular vehicle inspections such as once a year. You probably don't want to drive back every year at a certain time to take care of the inspection. Some states also charge a tax on the value of your vehicle when you register it. Usually you will get a credit for sales or use tax paid to the prior state, but not always. It's always a good idea to check out driver's license regulations, and how long they are good for, and if you can handle license and vehicle renewals through the mail. Most of the information can be found on an individual state's website.

Insurances such as Health, RV and Vehicle Insurances are also important to look into before choosing a state. Get some quotes from insurance agencies in your chosen state. If you happen to have your health insurance under a government program or retirement program where your state of residence doesn't matter, then it will be a lot easier. The Affordable Care Act made health insurance affordable for many, but was also more challenging for some Full-Time RVers depending on the state they lived in. It's wise to check your health insurance rates based on different states to get the best plan for the best price. You may also want to seek out a national system of "in network" health providers so that your coverage is "portable" from state to state. This website may also be helpful in your search for health insurance - www.rverhealthinsurance.com

Escapees RV Club also has mail forwarding services in the three favorite states of Florida, South Dakota, and Texas, and they are very helpful in explaining all the details to Full-timers. The club has many membership benefits, but there are extra fees for the mail forwarding service. See www.escapees.com for more details.

Why we chose South Dakota as our legal domicile

Since my husband and I were leaving California, and had no plans to return there to live, we decided to look for a state that was the easiest and one of the least expensive states. South Dakota came out on top for us. First, to establish the state as our legal domicile, we found a mail forwarding service in South Dakota, and there are several to choose from. The one we chose was recommended by a fellow RVer, located in Madison in the eastern part of South Dakota. In hindsight, I may have chosen a mail forwarding service in one of the larger cities in SD like Rapid City or Sioux Falls, but Madison is a college town, on a lake, and very quiet and rural so it has been nice to call Madison, our home base.

Mount Rushmore National Memorial in South Dakota

After we established ourselves with the mail forwarding service, we received our address with our own private mail box (PMB) number. We now get in touch with the service by phone or via email. The mail forwarding service will send your mail to any location that you give them which could be where you're staying at a campground or a relative's home. In addition, you can set up the mail forwarding based on your own preferences such as weekly, biweekly, and monthly. The mail service also can help you with registering your vehicles, and recommending local insurance companies for your vehicles.

Once we secured our mailing address which we arranged while we were still in California, then we stopped in Madison, SD, and stayed for a couple of nights. All you need to do to get your driver's license and register your vehicles is to get a PMB for your local address, and to stay in SD for one night, showing proof of your stay with either a receipt from your hotel or from your campground. Then go to the Division of Motor Vehicles (DMV) in SD http://dor.sd.gov/Motor_Vehicles/ to take care of your driver's license and vehicle registration. The mail forwarding service also helped us with the DMV paperwork. The driver's licenses are good for five years, and then you would need to return in person, but you can handle vehicle registrations, and insurances through the mail. (The state of SD now requires you to sign a Residency Affidavit which you also bring to the DMV.)

Ahead of time, we also contacted a local insurance agent for the vehicle insurances including the truck and Fifth Wheel, and to determine what the property tax would be on both. The rates were very good, and reasonable, especially compared to California.

The main reason we return to South Dakota every year has been for the health insurance. Being only in our 50s, and not having any other health insurance, we chose insurance through the Affordable Care Act, and it has been a great insurance plan. www.AveraHealthPlans.com in Sioux Falls, SD is our company, and the doctors and services have been outstanding. Avera is one of the companies in SD that didn't have any issues with Full-time RVers. The way health care is changing, it's hard to say what the future will hold. We've only traveled back to SD once each year to see our primary doctors, and coordinated our trips around the country to pass through SD. We've also been able to have questions answered, prescriptions filled, etc. while we've been living on the road. We haven't had any major health issues, but for those who are 65 and older, you probably could handle your health insurance needs through Medicare, and with a supplemental health insurance plan. If you're under 65, then it does take some shopping around for the best plan.

After choosing South Dakota, we actually considered switching to Florida when we were looking at buying property there, but between their rule of having to live in the state for six months and a day along with the higher vehicle insurance rates, we decided to stay with South Dakota. We didn't really look into Texas, but with the Escapees RV Club based in Texas, they would be a big help in assisting with locating your domicile to their state.

Returning to South Dakota every year has begun to feel like returning "home." We still sightsee around South Dakota, visiting sites like the Corn Palace with artwork entirely made out of corn, and the Wall Drug Store, a wonderland of western art and photo collections with a restaurant and unique retail outlets. The incredible national memorial and parks of that state have also made it well worth our time to visit every year. We have our favorite campgrounds, and our memorable experiences like driving right through Sturgis, SD during the 75th annual Biker's Rally in 2015. The entertaining tale of that adventure is next.

A Wildlife Adventure - Milestone 75th Anniversary of Sturgis Motorcycle Rally

An unexpected surprise was getting to experience the Sturgis Motorcycle Rally firsthand. Jim and I didn't plan on going to that event. It wasn't on our Bucket List. As we planned our route leaving Montana, we decided to head first to North Dakota, and then drive down to South Dakota to visit the Rapid City area, and then onto our official hometown of Madison, SD.

After arriving in North Dakota, we visited the Theodore Roosevelt National Park (NP), getting to experience their badlands along with more wildlife than we expected including bison, pronghorn, mule deer, prairie dog families and the first pack of wild horses that I have ever seen in a national park. After Yellowstone NP, this park was a refreshing change – a lot quieter with room to spread out.

As I watched the pack of wild horses, there were only a few other sight-seers. The wild horses in their many shades of beauty stood in a circle on a raised, flat rock. A striking white horse, the leader of the pack stood facing us, keeping an eye on the people who circled below. With a shake of his mane, the other horses followed his every command. At one point, all the horses stood facing away from the people with their tails swishing in the breeze while their leader stood guard stamping his foot and staring anyone down who got too close. Sitting on a bench, I watched in awe of these wild animals. Still roaming free over the open plains, I imagined what it must have been like a few hundred years ago when there were so many packs of wild animals living across this wide expanse of a country. The Native Americans seemed to have had more respect for the wild animals, and the earth, only hunting what they needed, and leaving no trace of their camps behind.

At least, we have these national parks, created by men and women with foresight like Theodore Roosevelt. The national park dedicated to his memory also covered some of his history, and how Roosevelt first came to the west to hunt bison, but then over time, he came to see the Wild West differently. No longer was it his private hunting grounds, but a place that he wanted to protect and preserve so that future generations could visit, and see what America had once been – a wild and naturally beautiful land.

As I left North Dakota behind with its fields of sunflowers and stacked bales of hay, I had no idea that I would be experiencing another kind of wild life in Sturgis. Sturgis is a tiny town in western South Dakota on the outskirts of the more famous Rapid City, known for the Mount Rushmore National Memorial. With a year-round population of less than 7,000 people, Sturgis is invaded every year for a week in August with bikers from all over the country, and perhaps the world. This year being the 75th anniversary, the number of bikers soared from a hundred thousand to close to a million. They basically took over all of western South Dakota even spreading out into the area around Devil's Tower in Wyoming.

As Jim drove the Bighorn RV on straight, but bumpy roads alongside farmlands, he decided to look for a smoother route. The trusty Rand McNally GPS unbeknown to us re-routed us so we were now heading through Sturgis, and then onto Rapid City. Under sunny skies, we cruised along until we arrived at the outskirts of Sturgis, then the bikers increased in numbers. Following the GPS route, it then dawned on us that the route was going right through the heart of Sturgis on the last Friday afternoon of the bike rally. At first, I gazed in all directions caught up in the excitement of being smack in the middle of Sturgis. Tents lined the streets, selling all kinds of wares from t-shirts to shot glasses and of course, all the biking accessories you could imagine. I wanted to stop and shop, buying some eye-popping souvenirs. But riding in a truck trailing a 39 foot Fifth Wheel, there aren't a lot of parking spaces in a small town that fit that big of a rig. As we creeped into town, the road-side stands grew in numbers and diversity, now serving all kinds of fast food along with Jack Daniels, and beer, of course. People-watching was also a sport here with the bikers and the biker chicks, some wearing a bare minimum of clothes. Black leather was the ruling fashion statement, but there were more ways to wear leather than I had imagined. From hot pants to mini-skirts, and from leather pasties to all-leather bras, I realized I didn't have the right outfit for this event.

As we neared the main intersection, that's when it got really interesting. The traffic lights were working, but there was little regard for the lights by the pedestrians who kept pouring across the street in their eye-catching outfits. Every time, the light changed, more people kept crossing. After having enjoyed the spectacle up to this point, I now grew anxious, wondering how we were going to make a left turn at the lights. I yelled to Jim, "I'll jump out and stop the traffic."

Getting ready to release my seat belt, Jim reached across with his arm, pinning me to the seat. "No way are you going out there in the middle of that crowd!"

"How else are we going to make the turn? These people aren't stopping for anyone," I said, tugging at my seatbelt.

There also seemed to be no police in sight. With big events, most towns would have police directing the traffic, but the Sturgis police probably had their hands full keeping all the bikers in line to bother with directing traffic.

Finally, a kind person coming the other direction, motioned for us to turn, and the stream of bikers parted, gaping at the size of our Fifth Wheel RV. I'm sure they were wondering who would be crazy enough to drive a huge RV through Sturgis on a Friday afternoon during bike week. I certainly wouldn't have chosen that route on purpose, but it turned out to be one of the most thrilling Friday afternoons on my trip around the country. I got to see the motorcycle rally up close and personal, and actually survived to tell the tale.

After that titillating drive through town, Jim and I headed to our campground on the outskirts of Rapid City. Lucky for us, we ended up having bikers for neighbors at the campground who regaled us with all the tales of Sturgis. It wasn't like you could escape the bikers. They were all over western South Dakota, taking in the famous sights of Mount Rushmore, the Badlands and the Wind Caves. Driving through the Needles, a narrow, winding route perfectly suited for thrilling bike rides. A constant stream of bikers drove by our campground, day and night. At first, it sounded like bumble bees, and then, as the bikers got closer and increased in numbers, the sound grew to a roaring cloud of locusts.

Having arrived at the end of bike week, the number of bikers dwindled after the week-end. A few hung around to see the sights, but most started heading out right after Sunday. The license plates in our campground included states from east to west. Our camping neighbors were a couple probably close to sixty from Wisconsin who had driven their new Toy Hauler with their motorcycle tucked inside like precious cargo to take in the special anniversary week of Sturgis. Without their biking outfits, they looked like any other Midwestern couple nearing retirement age. But when they donned their leather outfits with dark sunglasses to ride into Sturgis, they seriously turned into a Badass-looking couple. I was impressed, and it made me even miss my own tamer leather outfits packed away in the storage shed.

Every night that week, the couple would sit out at their picnic table, smoking and drinking beer. Jim and I joined them a couple of nights, sipping our white wine with cheese and crackers. We were certainly from different backgrounds, but I relished their tales of biking, and their plans for the future. They envied our house-free lifestyle of roaming around the country. They were in the midst of getting their homestead ready to sell, and looking forward to RVing in the southern states over the winter. Tom, the husband, said, "I'm so done with winters in Wisconsin," adding, "If it wasn't for the grandkids, I wouldn't live there anymore." They planned on buying a smaller home near their children – something I often heard from retired couples on the road. They'd sell the large home with all the surrounding acres to downsize to a smaller home often in retirement communities, or near their children. Then, they'd head out on the open highway with their RVs, fitting in all the famous sights before they got too old to venture far from home.

After a week in Rapid City, it was time to head to the eastern part of South Dakota to visit Madison, our hometown, to take care of some business. Leaving Sturgis behind, I had to buy a few souvenirs to remember such a memorable time. I didn't get to experience Sturgis from the back of a bike, but I did get to be a voyeur for a week, peeking in at a lifestyle of freedom-loving bikers on Harleys and decked out in their finest leather. It may not be my lifestyle choice, but I do admire their rebel spirits. Just another adventure in Living the RV Lifestyle.

Moving into your New RV Home and What to Pack for Life on the Road

After you've sold your home, or even if you're still in the process of selling your home, it can be helpful to begin moving items into your new RV home. My husband and I had three months to move in, and set up our RV for our first big trip around the country. We parked in the driveway of my family's home, and slowly organized our belongings, and got used to all the different systems of the RV which can take some time. We had never owned an RV before so of course, it will be easier for those who've vacationed with RVs for years.

The key point is to travel light. In our big move from California, we did ship our belongings east, and stored them in a shed, labeling boxes for the RV. After we purchased our RV, we had a stack of boxes to go through, deciding again if we really needed all those items. Life on the road is more casual so I left behind most of my dressy clothes, and packed more spring/summer clothes because I planned on traveling through states in the warmer weather. As it turned out, I did experience some wintry weather in that first year, and had to buy some warmer clothes like sweaters, and a winter coat in Louisiana which was really more of a rain coat with a lining. That was one of my lessons that first year – the weather can be very changeable wherever you travel so packing a winter coat is a wise decision for most Full-time RVers.

I also had to downsize my book collection, not easy for a writer, and for those of us who are working on the road. Kindle and other E-readers are great for the road, especially for novels, and light reading, but any kind of research books, I still like having the paperback version. So I whittled my on-board collection of books to about 12 books, along with a box of my own books to sell which I ended up carrying in the second vehicle when my car joined our traveling caravan on the road.

As far as kitchen items, we brought too many of those items the first year, and had to ship items back. Our dishware turned out to be too heavy, so we went and bought a lighter set of dishes, similar to Corelle dishware. We also cut down the number of dishes to a set of four including glasses and coffee cups. Plastic glasses are now sold BPA free so you may even want to invest in some of those. It turned out that we didn't entertain in the RV a whole lot, but more outdoor entertaining where paper dishes, and plastic cups are fine. Most RVers like to socialize at their picnic tables so a gas grill, and a cooler might also be handy for entertaining with your neighbors. Some people who love to cook may need more cooking devices than us, but we still suggest carrying the minimum because weight is an issue for the RV once you're moving around the country.

RV cleaning supplies are also important to bring along for your mobile home. With more sensitive pipes and plumbing, you don't want to use harsh cleaning products especially drain cleaners, bleach products, and toilet bowl cleaners. For cleaning your toilet bowl, buy a cleaning product especially made for RVs. (Scott toilet tissue is also safe for most RVs, and not as expensive as the products sold at the RV stores.) For cleaning your shower and sink, Dawn dish detergent works with its ability to breakdown oil. For all the details on taking care of your RV, check your owner's manual for your rig. If you take care of it properly from the outside to the inside, your RV will last a lot longer, and look good, too. There are companies that detail RVs like cars which can keep the outside of your rig from oxidizing, and losing its shiny finish. You can also learn how to do it yourself with the right cleaning products and a professional buffer.

You may also want to customize the RV to your own needs. We had a pull-out couch and we only used it for one guest that first year, so we swapped it out for a desk which is now where I write a lot easier than on the kitchen table. A blow-up air mattress can make a nice guest bed if you need one. We also took out two of the kitchen chairs that we weren't using a lot, and added a small desk chair. We also bought a light-weight metal filing cabinet where we store our important papers. (There is a list of important papers to bring along in the Resource section at the end of this book.) You may find that you have different desires like needing a workspace for beading, or making puzzles. The more comfortable you feel with the arrangement of your living space, then, the more you'll enjoy the journey.

My husband happens to like wood-working and he's a handy man, so he brought a lot of tools for "just in case" situations. But after the first year, he had to leave some behind including our portable generator. Those who like to go boondocking may want to have a back-up generator on hand. In our first year on the road, we mainly stayed in campgrounds with full hook-ups, or at least electricity. In Chapter 9, I write more about RV camping options including boondocking. Jim's lists of Essential Tools and Supplies, and Suggested Gear are in the Resource section at the end of the book.

Outdoor furniture is also nice, but go easy on the extra chairs and tables unless you're staying put in one place for a while. We've seen some elaborate outdoor furniture on the road from canopies to patio mats, and all kinds of chairs, and tables and decorations. They all add weight so again choose wisely. We found two foldable chairs, and a lounge chair with a small table to be plenty. We also have a sun screen which attaches to the awning, and a patio mat which we use occasionally, and ended up carrying in our second vehicle to eliminate the weight from the RV.

Outdoor sports gear is also going to be a personal choice. We brought along our bicycles, and actually used them, but don't cart them around unless you really plan on biking. That goes for those kayaks that many people bring, and seldom use. They do have some nice, light-weight kayaks that can be easier to carry. We brought our beach and hiking accessories because we love to do both, but didn't bring golf clubs, tennis racquets, snow or water skis, fishing gear, etc. If you really want those items, then bring them along, but you may also be able to rent them at different places that you stay.

As far as bringing along exercise equipment, our best decision was to join a gym that has facilities around the country. Our choice was Anytime Fitness, a 24/7 gym with locations around the country, and around the world. It has been worth every penny on the road. With so much sitting while you're traveling, it always felt good to find a gym in a new location, and also made me feel more at home. The Anytime Fitness gyms always have nautilus, free weight equipment and aerobic equipment; and some offer classes either live or on video. The gyms have to meet a set standard so some are simpler and others have more of the extras like great showers, and towels included. The other "around the country" gyms we've seen are Planet Fitness and Gold's Gym, but check them out for yourself. Since being on the road, I've been able to stay in shape so it's been well worth the monthly fee. I do have an exercise mat, and some exercise bands for when I'm in between gyms, but walking, hiking and biking have been great exercise as well.

Other extra items that have been worth their added weight, are our air cleaner. Smells are stronger in a smaller space. In colder or hotter weather, you may not want to open your windows. Since the first day we left, we brought along our air cleaner, mainly for the bedroom area to keep it fresh, but also as a sound machine to drown out unwanted sounds at night. Once you've stayed in as many campgrounds as us, you'll discover that they're not always built in quiet areas. They are often on the side of highways, and for some reason, some have trains that go by at all hours of the night. A battery-operated sound machine when you don't have electricity also comes in handy at those free camping nights at Wal-Mart and casinos where it's not always quiet even at midnight.

Another item that we added the second year was a Reverse Osmosis water filter system which fits nicely under the kitchen sink. My husband installed it following the directions, but it could probably also be installed at an RV shop. After a year of traveling, and only using a Brita water filter pitcher, we were ready to make sure that we were drinking the purest of water wherever we happened to be camping. It is definitely worth it, and there is still room under the sink for cleaning supplies. Water filtering options can be found at www.rvwaterfilterstore.com.

Surprisingly, one of the heaviest items in the RV was the original queen size mattress that came with the Bighorn RV. In keeping with lightening our load, my husband decided to order a Sleep Number mattress made especially for RVs which is an adjustable air mattress. I did miss my comfortable bed from my traditional house, which now rested inside the storage shed. The message from my bed story following this section would be: Make sure you find a comfortable, light-weight bed, hopefully, before you leave the driveway. If you can live with a queen size, great, but if a king-size will only do, then it will cost you some space in the bedroom. There are some concessions to be made down-sizing into a smaller space. You do have to leave some of that extra stuff behind for safety on the road, and also, because you just don't have room for it all. One of the realities of living in an RV: You are now living in a Tiny Home, and sometimes, that means adjusting to a new bed.

A Sleepless Adventure - When did I become the Princess Sleeping on the Pea?!

The search for a comfortable bed had become almost laughable. Like the princess who could feel a pea under her stack of mattresses, I had Jim order a variety of pillow top covers for the bed with none feeling as plushy as my former bed. Finally, we tossed the mattress that came with the RV into a landfill in Arizona. While other people remember Winslow, Arizona as the town made famous by the Eagles song, Take it Easy (written by Jackson Browne and Glenn Frey), I will remember Winslow as the final resting place of my RV mattress.

Jim and Donna Standing on the Corner in Winslow, Arizona

My new Sleep Number mattress made specifically for RV homes arrived at the Meteor Crater campground in Arizona where we stayed that week. My sister, Doreen happened to be visiting that memorable week, touring around the national parks with us. In between visiting the Grand Canyon, Petrified Forest, and Sedona, my bed arrived. Anticipating a good night's sleep after a rocky three months on the road, I collapsed onto the bed, experimenting with the range of sleep numbers. Beginning at a higher number closer to 100, I quickly lowered the firmness of the mattress until I was only left with number 5. The bed didn't go any lower, and it still felt too firm for me. I had become the princess sleeping on a pea.

After spending all that money on a new queen-size bed, I

couldn't justify buying another one so I piled back on all the pillow top covers until I sunk into a cushy crevice. Now, I sleep on one side of the bed with a hump in the middle while Jim sleeps on his side at his favorite sleep number. We both miss our soft-sided king size waterbed. Perhaps, there is no bed that matches the comfort of our former bed. I can only think of one bed more comfortable, and that was a feather bed at the Hotel Windsor in Melbourne, Australia where the English royalty stayed when they were in town. I guess I need a bed fit for a King and a Queen.

As you can see, I am not really roughing it on this grand circle of the country. As I tell people on the road, I am not on a camping trip or even a summer vacation, this is my lifestyle now. If this is going to be my only home, I want to be comfortable. In the past, I gazed at those long, luxurious RVs, and scoffed that that wasn't really camping. Now, I understand why they were living in those wheel estates. They, too, had probably progressed from the tiny tent to the pop-up camper, and then to the van camper, and finally upgraded into their 40 foot plush palace. Once you've lived in one of these comfortable caravans, it's hard to go back to sleeping on the ground in a tent with morning dew dripping on your face. That may be fine in your 20's, but in your 50's and older, comfort is what a King and a Queen need on the road.

Chapter 4

Transition Time: Leaving your Traditional Life behind for Living in an RV

In the midst of this busy time in your life, you probably haven't had a lot of time to reflect on what this big change will mean for your life. Once, you make the decision, and begin the process of getting ready for the RV journey, there is so much to do that you can keep busy and not have to think about the impact of this change on your life.

Being a counselor, I'm familiar with how big changes can affect people. First, you begin to think about the change, and then work through the issues such as listing the pros and cons of your pending decision. Then, this big decision may begin to affect you emotionally especially as you go through the belongings of your home, deciding what to keep, and what to let go of. You may begin to feel the impact of this decision which can bring up sadness and loss. Letting go of your home, your community, and your whole lifestyle as you've known it is huge.

Like any loss, you can find yourself going through the stages of grief – Denial (This isn't really that big. I've moved before.); Anger (How did I let my husband/wife convince me to do this?!); Bargaining (We can always come back and visit our old hometown.); Depression (I miss my old life, my home, my family, my friends.); and hopefully, you'll get to Acceptance (I finally am enjoying my new lifestyle of Full-time RVing.)

The timetable is different for everyone. We all go through loss in our own way. Some of us will keep looking in the rear view mirror until we start to see the new road ahead.

My husband and I did go through this whole process differently. He was ready to let go of his corporate career, and kept busy with all the arrangements of moving cross country, and handling our family estates. I had a harder time with the move. First, there was the leaving of California where we had lived for 17 years, leaving behind a dream home that I loved along with my home-based counseling business, and a community of friends and neighbors that had become like family.

As I prepared to leave California behind, I was still grieving the loss of my parents who passed away within a couple of years of each other. I was heading back to Cape Cod to my family home to help with the process of getting it ready for my sister to move into. I was also helping Jim with the loss of his last parent, and getting his family homes ready to sell. For me, the losses kept piling up. I thought I was dealing with them one at a time, but the busyness of selling homes, and moving kept me occupied.

The losses caught up with me once my husband and I headed out on the highway for our new Full-time RVing life. Jim was excited to leave his corporate life behind, and to live a freer lifestyle. I wasn't quite ready to give up my work, and tried to continue my counseling work over the phone, and in person when I could, but it was challenging. It probably took me about six months to get used to living on the road. Returning to California on our trip around the country helped a great deal to re-connect with all of our friends, and have an Open House at our new Bighorn home. Once, we left there, I began to find a rhythm with my new lifestyle.

My message would be to not downplay how big this lifestyle change can be. Many of you are going through similar changes such as retiring from life-long careers, selling businesses as well as homes, and moving away from your support systems of family and friends. There are many ways to stay in touch on the road with cell phones, internet, and occasional visits in person. You'll develop your own rhythm in time, and your own community of support on the road. What also helped me is knowing that I would continue this Full-time RV lifestyle as long as it was enjoyable and working for both of us. At some point, we could always go back to a traditional lifestyle. Full-time RVing doesn't have to be a forever choice. In the final chapter, I talk about having an exit strategy for the future. My personal story at the beginning of the RV journey is next.

The Adventure Begins - Preparing for the Trip of a Lifetime

It's now about six weeks before I will be starting my new lifestyle on the road. I have been waking up over the years in traditional homes, but in the coming year, I will be moving all around this incredible country. I will be waking up in different places from a month's stay to a few weeks, and in some places, only a one night-stand.

Honestly, I am anxious about this journey on the road. I waver between excitement to what was I thinking?! I am traveling with my new RV home. Like a turtle with his shell on his back, I am bringing my home with me. It will be my only home. I don't have a home to go back to. This is it – my turtle shell. I am sharing this shell with my husband who happens to be a Cancer, the astrology sign of the crab. I think he may be more comfortable with this idea of living in a shell. I am a Libra, and enjoy living in a peaceful and beautiful space. I am certain that I will find some of those spaces on the road, but then I wonder about those nights, spent in the Wal-Mart parking lot, or a few miles away from the Mardi Gras celebration of New Orleans. Will I find peace and beauty in those moments?! I will have to dig deep into my personal tool box for self-help tools and resources, and remember to be present with all that is happening and unfolding around me in the moment.

In this coming year, I know I will be challenged and stretched out of my comfort zone. I also know that I will be held spellbound by the immensity and beauty of this great country that I live in. From the rolling, emerald hills, to the stark, sandy deserts, and from the Atlantic to the Pacific, and everything in between, I know I will be marveling at the scenery of this country. I know I will treasure those simple moments of having breakfast in a diner in the Midwest, to eating alfresco by the Gulf of Mexico. I will relish hearing all those different accents, and laugh when they try to pinpoint my own New England accent especially when they see the South Dakota plates on my vehicles.

In time, I will find a way to share my story of where I came from, and how I ended up on this cross-country journey, feeling too young to be considered a retiree, and too old to be traveling around the country to find myself. I have spent years finding myself, and know that it has nothing to do with where you're living. The self-discovery journey is definitely an inner journey, and the one, I will be taking this coming year is an outer journey, but who knows?! It may be a combination of both.

Buffalo in Yellowstone National Park in Wyoming, Idaho and Montana

Chapter 5

RV Basics - Before you go

Before you're ready to travel around the country, you need to go over some of the RV Basics to make sure that you're really ready for RV life on the road. Ask yourself these questions:

- ✓ Are you comfortable with driving your new RV and backing it into a campsite?
- ✓ Do you know how to easily hitch/unhitch your RV; or if you're towing another vehicle, how to take it off its trailer, or unhitch it from the RV?
- ✓ Are you comfortable connecting your utilities at a full hook-up camp site which usually includes electric, water, sewer, and possibly cable and/or satellite?
- ✓ What about your plumbing system and the holding tanks – the fresh water tank, the gray tank for the kitchen sink, bathroom sink and shower; and the black water tank for the toilet – do you know how these operate and how to empty them, and maintain them?
- ✓ Do you know how all your appliances work including the refrigerator, stove/oven, microwave, fireplace, etc.?
- ✓ What about the condition of your tires on your RV, and your truck and tow-behind vehicle? Do you have the right tire pressure? If you bought your RV used, how many miles do you have left on the tires? (Seven years is the limit on most RV tires.)
- ✓ Do you know how the heating system works, and how to get your propane tanks filled?

- ✓ Do you understand your electrical system, both AC and DC operation including the generator?

All of these questions are important for anytime RVing, but especially for Full-time RVing. If you don't know the answers to these questions on your particular RV, there are a few good ways to find them out. Your local RV shop or a national chain like Camping World can be helpful in doing a thorough maintenance check on your RV, and even going over how the RV works. If you bought it new, then ask all those questions, and have someone give you a comprehensive tour of your RV before you drive it off the lot.

Other places to learn about your RV are at specific events that are held for newbies, and Full-timers who want a refresher course on the road. Escapees RV Club www.escapees.com offers rallies around the country, but the best event for learning all these topics is their RVers' BootCamp which specifically focuses on RV maintenance and operation; Towing, tire and weight safety; and Basic RV systems. We didn't attend the BootCamp, but are members of the Escapees and it's been a great way to learn about RVing as well as get discounts at their campgrounds, and other affiliated campgrounds.

Other learning opportunities are at the rallies that Howard and Lynda Payne of www.RV-Dreams.com run usually twice a year for newbies who may not even have an RV yet, and other Full-timers who want to learn the ropes. They cover all the topics from the beginning steps of first choosing your RV, and all the way through the care of your RV; and how to make it work financially by workamping/volunteering and all the camping options that are out there. My husband and I never attended their rallies, but they sound extremely helpful, and they get good reviews from other Full-timers. The Paynes have been Full-timing since 2005 when they headed out on the road at age 41. They continue to work and travel around North America, and must have a wealth of knowledge and experience on RVing which they seem to enjoy sharing with others.

If you're more the adventurous type, and learn by doing, another good way is to go camping at a local campground. It's something I've noticed at campgrounds around the country, people trying out their new RV at a campground close to home. They'll usually stay for a week-end or longer, just enough time to get a feel for all the systems, and get some practice with the driving, hitching/unhitching, and hooking up all the utilities. Camp Hosts can be a good resource and give you some good advice so look for a campground with a friendly staff if you want to take on this learning method. Fellow RVers in the park are usually willing to offer help as well.

Our learning method was to learn from the seller of our Bighorn RV who was very meticulous, and took his time explaining everything and how it worked. He also gave us some great check-lists for opening and closing the RV which are in the Resource section at the end of the book. We also learned a great deal by living in my family's driveway for three months and actually running all the systems. My husband also learned a lot on-line about the RV Basics, and by searching YouTube for some helpful videos including one on backing up which really helped him get the hang of backing up a truck with an RV that is nearly as long as some tractor trailer trucks on the highway.

In hindsight, I think Jim would have enjoyed a driving school experience, but there were no schools close to our starting point on Cape Cod so he learned by doing. With such a long RV, and truck, he kept to highways mainly at first, and looked for campgrounds that weren't too far off the beaten path. We would often find the campground, and set up, and then take the truck sight-seeing. Later when we had our second vehicle, it made it even easier to visit cities, and places where dually trucks don't park so easily. In Zion National Park in Utah, we even had to pay an extra fee for our dually to allow us to go through the tunnel on the east entrance. My husband joked, "I knew my wide ass was going to cost me someday." Down the road, a second vehicle could save you some of that hassle as well as save on fuel.

Sandstone layers near the East entrance of Zion National Park

Chapter 6

Staying Safe with your RV

Being safe on the road as you travel around the country is so important for yourself, and for others on the highway. In my travels around the country, I've seen some bad accidents with RVs off the side of the road into trees, and other times, ripping their roof and awnings off with low-hanging tree branches. Driving an RV of any kind takes extra attention and awareness on the road. We all tend to get comfortable with our everyday vehicles, cruising along and not always actively thinking about our driving. You can NOT do that when you're driving your RV. To be safe out on the road, you need to give it your 100% attention which means no eating lunch, no cell phones, and absolutely no texting. Of course, there will be times when you get distracted by your driving partner, by traffic, or even by your pets, but taking your eye off the road for a few seconds can be devastating.

Some of the tools that can help you with staying safe out there on the highway could be getting some driving lessons for driving your big rig. Some people are naturally better at driving large vehicles. They may also have had previous experience, driving delivery trucks and school buses. But if you haven't driven anything bigger than a car or small truck, then you may want to look into the lessons and/or practice in an empty parking lot or field. Set up some cones, and keep practicing, taking those wide turns, backing up (without your towed vehicle), and maneuvering into parking spaces like at a rest area or truck stop. You'll feel a lot more comfortable out on the road with some practice.

Another key safety factor that I've mentioned before is NOT overloading your RV. Travel as light as you can. You'd be surprised at what all those clothes, extra dishes, and extra gadgets/appliances can weigh. If you can get your RV weighed the first year on the road, you'll have a better idea of how you're doing with weight, and make adjustments. Every truck and RV has a weight limit, find it out, and try to tow/pack less than that weight. SmartWeigh is a service offered by Escapees RV Club www.escapees.com at some of their campgrounds. It's well worth staying at one of their Rainbow Parks, and getting your rig weighed. If you're overloaded and get in an accident, you may be held responsible for the accident because of the weight of your RV. In the long run, it's worth it to travel with less weight.

Another important safety item is taking care of the tires on your truck and RV. Your tires are the foundation of your RV home. Make sure they are in good shape, and are at the right tire pressure. My husband bought a tire monitoring system for the RV tires which lets you know if a tire is losing pressure. It's so important to check your tires at every stop, just by handling them to see if they are too hot, or losing pressure. If you get a blow-out on an RV tire, it can really ruin the undercarriage of your rig, and not to mention, spoil your whole trip. Take time to check your tire pressure whenever you've been moving around a lot on the road.

Another tool worth investing in is a GPS for RVers. Jim bought the Rand McNally GPS for RVs, and I'm sure there are other brands on the market as well. Some of the features on the Rand McNally version took some getting used to, but it was very helpful for planning your route, and knowing you'd be alerted if you encountered low bridges, or tunnels where carrying propane is not allowed. When you first set up the GPS, you plug in the specifications for your rig such as height, weight, length, and whether or not, you're carrying propane. Then you can set up your preferences such as staying off dirt roads, avoiding U-turns, or not taking ferries. When you plan your route on the GPS, then it will automatically select a travel route according to your preferences, and avoiding bridges that are too low, or tunnels where you can't carry propane. You can also extend the travel time of your trip if you know you'll be making more stops, or driving slower than the posted speed limit which isn't a bad idea. Many of the cross-country highways have speed limits as high as 80 mph or more, but when you're driving an RV, it's usually better for safety and gas mileage to drive closer to 65 mph. When you're Full-timing, you don't have to be in a hurry, and getting there safely is certainly a lot more important than arriving at a certain time.

Many of the newer RVs have rear and side cameras that can make it a lot easier to back up your rig. If your rig doesn't have any camera, then you may want to invest in at least the rear camera. It can make a big difference especially if you're driving solo, and don't have anyone to guide you into a space. Some campground hosts will help guide you into a campsite, but some, will only hand you a map, and you're on your own. If you have a driving partner, using walkie-talkies (two-way radios) can also be helpful when you're backing into a tight campsite. Many of the state parks and national parks don't have the largest campsites, and you can often find yourself having to back into a tight space with lots of trees around. Those cameras can be a big plus along with having a companion to help guide you into the space. Don't forget to look up for any low-hanging tree branches or wires. Don't be afraid to ask for help from the campground, or even your neighbors. Dash cameras are also popular these days, and a good accessory if you happen to be involved in an accident where there is some question on who is at fault. It's not a necessary tool, but some drivers feel better having one.

Fire safety is also an issue that you need to be aware of living in an RV. It's so important to have your fire extinguishers on board and up to date. It's also wise to NEVER use candles in your RV. Luckily, there are LED candles now sold that look so real – some are even made out of wax, and have flickering lights. When it comes to campfires, make sure your campfire is as far away as possible from the RV and any other flammable objects like your camp chairs, towels, bikes, etc.

Since living in California with the threat of wildfires, I haven't been able to enjoy a camp fire as much in the hotter and drier climates. When you are going to have a campfire, make sure that there are no burn bans, and that it isn't too windy. Only have a campfire within a circle of rocks, or a specific container made for fires like a fire pit. If possible, surround the campfire with an area of dirt, or clear the area down to the ground. It seems like it would be common sense, but never leave the campfire unattended. Have a bucket of water, and small shovel nearby. When it's time to go to bed, or leave the campsite, make sure the fire is out. Dump lots of water on the fire, stir with a shovel, and then dump even more water. Make sure it's cold. If there are any embers still hot, douse with more water. Never leave a campfire with hot embers. It turns out that many of those California wildfires started from unattended campfires.

One of the best gifts that the seller of our Bighorn RV gave us were his check-lists for opening and closing the rig. "Opening" means setting up when you arrive at a campground, and then "closing" down when you're getting ready to leave, and head out on the highway. The check lists have saved us a few times when we forgot a key item. We still use the check lists every time we pack up to leave a campground, but maybe, not as often as when we set up. I've included the check lists in the

Resource section at the end of the book to give you an idea of what to add to your own personal check lists. The check lists can save you from driving off with your antennae or satellite dish still up in the air (which I've seen more than once), or from having your stairs still down. Both events could spoil your trip, and lead to a time out at the repair shop. In Chapter 11, I'll cover more about the mishaps and adventures of being a Full-time RVer. Know that you're not alone in breaking down at times, or needing a tow, but the more you can keep up with the RV maintenance, it will make your trip go a lot more smoothly. Be safe out there on the highway.

Chapter 7

Traveling with your Pets

Many people choose the RV lifestyle because they always wanted to travel with their pets. Some can't imagine going anywhere even on a cross-country trip without their pets. As I've traveled around the country, I've seen so many different breeds of dogs come bounding out of RVs – from Great Danes to tiny Terriers. Sometimes, I've seen people walking three or four dogs around the campground, and head back to their RV where they all piled onboard.

The RV lifestyle can work for many dogs, and even other pets, but it's probably wise to take some test runs with your pet to see how much they enjoy traveling. Some dogs ride all the time with their owners in their car, but it's still a good idea to take them on a week-end trip first in the RV to see how they do, and what they might need.

Some of the essentials are a collar with name tags (even if the pet does have a microchip), a harness, and a couple of different leashes – a shorter, four-to-six foot one for busy areas, and a longer, 10 – 20 foot retractable leash for open areas in the country, and at some campgrounds. All campgrounds seem to require that pets be on a leash at all times, and most don't tolerate animals being tied up outside the RVs except when you're sitting outside with them.

My husband worked as a Camp Host one summer season in Utah, and one of his biggest pet peeves (pardon the pun) was having to remind pet owners about keeping their pets on a leash at all times, and picking up their pet's poop. You would think that most people are used to those rules even where they live in more traditional neighborhoods, but it seems some people seem to "forget" the rules when there is no one around watching them.

Anyway, I've had the most fun taking my cat, Zeus out for a walk on a leash around the campgrounds. It seems that a lot of people have not ever seen a cat walking on a leash. Zeus is now 17 years old, and has been walking on a leash for about 7 years. His outdoor adventures began at my last home where he was mainly an indoor cat with an occasional outing on the back deck until I decided to try walking him and his brother on a leash. They were about 10 years old at the time so it did take some practice, but they quickly learned that this was the way to go outside. At the end of this chapter, I have included a story of Zeus' travels on the road.

Some campgrounds might insist on keeping your pets' vaccines up to date. Some do have you sign forms that attest to this fact, but it's best to bring along their health records, and extra supplies of their medications just in case of an emergency.

Other items that can make pet travel more comfortable are outdoor bedding, and indoor pet beds; outdoor exercise pens for smaller dogs; favorite toys; a collapsible crate or pet carrier; portable water dishes for hiking and long walks; pick-up bags; first aid kit; dog shampoo and brushes; flea and tick spray; muzzle; orange vest with reflectors for night walks, and hunting season; paw boots for rough terrain, hot sand and cold weather; and a life jacket for swimming and boating. If they have special food needs, you may want to stock up, but watch the weight in the RV. Those pet food cans, and large bags of dry food can add up fast.

Having your pet along can make you feel more at home especially as you transition to the Full-time life. My cat, Zeus has been a great companion and a comfort while we've traveled, and one lucky cat, to be able to see so many places in his lifetime. I think Zeus might have more than nine lives. Here's his story.

Zeus climbing a Black Willow tree

Pet Adventures – Traveling with My Cat, Zeus, the Road Warrior

Like John Steinbeck with his dog, Charley, Jim and I were

fortunate to have a traveling cat – not just a cat who tolerated traveling, but who seemed to even love it, more than me at times. In California, I never took my cats with me on vacations, or even on road trips. I always called up a friend, and later a pet sitter to keep an eye on my cats while I was away. I didn't think of bringing them with me because I usually stayed in hotels or resorts that didn't allow pets. I didn't realize that that was why many people traveled in RVs so that they could bring along their pets on summer vacations and week-end getaways.

When we finally sold our home in California in June 2014, we decided to drive back to Massachusetts, and take Zeus on his first major road trip. We had taken him away for a long week-end once, and he did well. But traveling cross-country was the big test. Zeus did better than I could have ever imagined. Most of the time, he quietly sat on my lap, or on the back seat, only getting antsy when he needed to eat or take a bathroom break. I even got out his leash, and walked him at rest areas if he wanted to go outside. At most campsites, Zeus couldn't wait to get out and sniff around just like all the dogs we saw at the campgrounds.

Eventually, we did see other cats. But most of the time, they stayed in their RVs, and slept in the big front windows of the Class A Mobile homes, or peeked out of windows in the Airstreams. Zeus also claimed his favorite spots in our RV – sitting atop his scratching post next to the dining room table, or on the back of the recliners, and even in the cubbyholes of the RV. He liked to try new spots so that he could have different views of the outdoors.

At first, Zeus didn't mind moving around every week, or two. But by the end of our first grand circle of the country, he started to grow tired of the constant moving. I could usually tell when he was sleeping on the bed, and opened one eye in the morning, and gave me a look on moving day. "Like you gotta be kidding! We're moving again. Didn't we just get here?" Okay, maybe, that was me speaking through Zeus.

I think Zeus was as happy as me to arrive on Cape Cod, and stay in my sister's driveway for a couple of months. Now, we've been staying in more places longer which gives him a chance to really get to know the campground even if the neighbors and their pets keep changing. At each campground where he's stayed longer, Zeus has created his walking routine which varies slightly, but most of the time, he checks out the same spots, usually ending up on the picnic table, waiting for a brushing. I guess cats are also creatures of habit. Right now, as I write about Zeus, he's waiting for his nightly walk. Morning and night, and sometimes mid-day, he ventures out, ready to see the new arrivals at the campground, and to check out the local birds.

Zeus' presence on this journey around the country has been a calming influence at times, and comforting when I've been moving around so much. His constant loving attention has been reassuring especially when I left behind many of those *creature comforts that make up a home. Living more simply was one thing, but living without Zeus was never an option. He's made the trip more entertaining even with his challenging moments. Zeus began this trip at age 14, and is still going strong at 17. I'm hopeful that Zeus will be with us into his 20's. Traveling wouldn't be the same without him.*

Chapter 8

Staying Connected on the Road

In the past, camping for most people was getting away from it all which included away from technology such as the television, the phone, and now, the internet. Some people still like to camp that way, but when it's your Full-time life, it's a different situation. Many people need to be connected for their jobs that travel with them, and others just love to stay connected with family, friends, and their on-line interests. Whatever your needs are, it's best to start with your cellular phone company for phone and internet.

Cell Phone and Internet options

The major cellular companies all have added special services to be able to connect with the internet through your cell phone. So if you already have a cell phone with a decent nation-wide phone plan, I would start with your own company, and then explore the others if need be. The phone companies are always coming up with new devices and plans so check as it gets closer to your time to head out on the highway.

My husband, and I had T-Mobile in California, and had a really good deal so we decided to stick with them. Since leaving California, we have encountered spotty areas for phone service like in the Midwest when T-Mobile's coverage isn't as good or non-existent, and it switches over to AT & T for phone service only. For the most part, we haven't stayed in those areas that long so we've been okay with the coverage. The monthly cost was still less expensive than the other major cellular providers.

We also now have T-Mobile hot spots through our Samsung phones that allow us a set amount of data every month for internet access. Using our mobile hot spots in our phones is the most secure way to connect with the internet on the road. If we're at a campground, we'll check out their Wi-Fi services first which sometimes require a password. In our RV, we use a device that we purchased called PepWave that takes the campground's Wi-Fi, and re-broadcasts it in our RV, creating our own private Wi-Fi network in the RV, and even amplifying a weak signal. This is good for doing internet searches and other activities that do not require a secure network. A savvy computer person could still hack into your personal computers through the campground Wi-Fi. If you're doing any financial transactions, or even private email, I would suggest using a mobile hot spot in your own cell phone before using a campground's Wi-Fi. A helpful website for learning about all these different options is www.RVMobileInternet.com.

Television options

Many campgrounds do provide cable television service, but not all campgrounds do. If you're going to be a Full-time RVer, most people like to have satellite television so that they don't need to rely on a campground. The most popular satellite dishes are mounted on the roof of your RV. These satellite dishes then automatically search for a signal when you turn them on in a new location. The only challenge is when there are trees or other objects that block the view of the satellite then you can have a problem. The rooftop dishes are also quite expensive, but a good investment if you plan on Full-timing for more than a couple of years. There are also satellite dishes that go on a tri-pod, and can be manually adjusted for the right angle. These are less expensive, and another option.

We opted for a Winegard satellite dish which looks like a white dome that is mobile so we can move it to different locations to get a better view of the satellite in the sky. It does not need to be set up on a tri-pod. Sometimes, it works fine on the ground, and other times, you have to move it to the top of the RV for the best signal. The Winegards can also be mounted as well. Our television provider is Direct-TV, and you can sign up for different plans just like in your traditional home that include basic channels, or add on the special movie channels. Each time, we move to a new location in another state, we do have to call Direct-TV and let them know that our location address has changed to be able to watch the local affiliate stations for channels like NBC, ABC, CBS, etc. We also have the DVR which allows us to record our favorite shows, and watch them later with or without commercials. Just like in homes, you can also have the DVR service on more than one television for an extra cost.

There is a Distant Network Service offered by Direct-TV for RVers. To sign up for the service, you do have to sign an affidavit that you are mobile and that your dish is attached to your rig. You also have to send a copy of your RV registration. With this plan, you cannot get true local channels (i.e. NBC, CBS, FOX, and ABC) in each community you visit, but you do get instead the New York or Los Angeles local channels which include the major networks. This service is only for mobile RVers. This is to keep people in traditional houses from bypassing their local TV channels in favor of New York and Los Angeles stations (local advertisers and TV stations don't like that.) With this plan, it does seem that you have to choose either the east or west coast for those "local" channels.

In our RV, we like to have the true local channels of the area that we're visiting so we can watch their local news and weather as well as the national news. It's also been great with the DVR to be able to tape wherever you are so you can watch television when it's convenient for you. After all, this is your life on the road, and it's nice to have a television as an entertainment option. It may be hard to imagine right now, but sometimes, you do get tired of sitting around the campfire toasting marshmallows, and watching the sunset.

The story below is one of our times on the road when we had what I call the three "deadlies" – No cell phone service, no internet, and no television. For some people, this may sound like heaven, and at times, it can be, but other times, it can feel quite isolating and downright scary. In this experience, it was one of several signs that it was time to settle down in one place for a season.

Another Camping Adventure – Follow the Signs

In November, I set my sights on visiting one more national park in our first year on the road. The Congaree NP was in South Carolina. I had only driven through a corner of the state on my way down to Florida last year. Jim had visited Myrtle Beach on the South Carolina coast years ago, and baked on the beach with all the other northerners celebrating the arrival of spring. This time, we drove inland to see one more national park before heading to Florida for the winter. It was one of the lesser known parks. I had only read about it in my guidebook.

The rain continued to dog us all the way to our destination, a state park campground. Once we drove off the highway, we followed a road which became narrow and more desolate. Without the sun, the November day appeared to be slipping away. Road weary, we plowed on through the gray mist. Finally, we saw a sign for the state park, and turned down a paved road that quickly turned to gravel and then to dirt. Since it was a weekday in late fall, no one manned the campground's guard shack. Jim had made the reservations on-line, and had a site number so we inched along, searching for the site. Without a lot of room to turn around, we didn't want to miss the reserved site. Finally, we found it almost at the end of the campground. I jumped out to help Jim back into an impossible site, and sunk into murky brownness. At this hour of dusk, everything appeared to be brown – the trees, the mud, and the road that led us there. We set up the RV as quickly as we could, and hunkered down inside for the night.

Once inside the RV, I nibbled on cheese and crackers, and noticed my cell phone wasn't working. There were no nearby cell towers. Being a state park, there was also no free WIFI which meant no internet access either without our cell phones working. Jim peeked out the door to see trees above, dripping moss and mosquitos – a size we had never seen before in New England. He could tell that meant no satellite reception as well for television. We had encountered the deadly three – no phones, no internet and no television. My heart skipped a beat as my mind scrambled to uncover all that could go wrong, deep in the woods. What if we had a medical emergency? What if we got stuck in all this mud? What if

Bigfoot came out of the woods? Other diehard campers lurked in the woods around us, but I wasn't so sure that they would open their door to a stranger.

The oppression of the dark, damp woods creeped into my home on wheels. It was one of those long, restless nights, listening to noises outside my window. Even when the sun came up the next morning, it was hard to tell if it was ever going to be light with all the creepy trees hanging overhead. By mid-morning, it appeared to be another rainy day. This was our last day left in South Carolina so we thought we better go find the Congaree National Park. And that's when we discovered what being lost really is.

The Congaree NP was once called, the Congaree Swamp National Monument. But in November, 2003, its status was changed to a national park, and the word, "swamp" was dropped from its title. After that, many more people stopped by to visit this national park hidden in the Deep South. It could have been because now it was officially a national park, or it might have been because it was no longer called a swamp. In either case, I only discovered this historical tidbit when I read my book on national parks.

I am still inclined to call it a swamp, but that might have something to do with how my journey to the park turned out.

This is how the day went. Jim and I decided to head for the national park because it would be our last one before arriving in Florida for the winter. We had been on this trip around the country for almost a year now, and seen over 30 national parks so what was one more?! With our trusty GPS, and Google maps, we had found places wherever we went. So we typed in Congaree's address, and proceeded to head there. Under gloomy skies, I thought it was probably the perfect day to visit a floodplain forest, the technical word for a swamp.

Heading out of the still dark forest, we drove towards the main road, and that's where the fun really began. Without a good signal for Google maps, we followed our Garmin GPS which almost always had gotten us to where we needed to go. This time was another story, but I am not sure I can even blame the Garmin. I don't think someone wanted us to find the Congaree NP.

Right away, we began to hit roadblocks, not the figurative ones, but the literal roadblocks - the sign on the road emblazoned across the metal and cement fence reading, "Roadblock" in large, black letters. There was no going around the sign. So we turned the car around, hoping the GPS would re-route, and so it did. And then we slammed into another "Roadblock" sign just like the other one. At first, I thought we got turned around, and we were back on the same road. But No, this was a different roadblock sign. And this is how it went for at least an hour or maybe longer. Somehow, you lose track of time when you're running into literal roadblocks. With a persevering nature, Jim wasn't giving up easily. While, I, on the other hand, started to believe that these signs might be more than just physical signs. Could it be a sign that today wasn't the day to visit Congaree? With New England stubbornness, we barreled on down the road. And lo and behold, we found the entrance to Congaree NP. By this time, we were so turned around that I couldn't tell you how we found it, or even where it was. The national park appeared out of the mists like a mirage.

In the parking lot, there was only one other vehicle. After all, it was a gray, November Monday which might be a redundant statement, but nonetheless, it was a national park on our list to see. With anticipation of buying pins, postcards and possibly t-shirts, we grabbed our raincoats, and headed to the front door. Peering through the dark glass, there didn't seem to be anyone in the store. That's when I read the sign on the door, "Closed Monday and Tuesday." Reeling back from the door, I stammered the words to Jim, "They are closed today and tomorrow." Every other national park we've visited had been open every day of the week, but not this one.

The Congaree NP did appear to still be open to visitors as long as you wanted to take a self-guided tour of the swamp in the rain. So that's what we did. Piling on more layers of rain gear, I drudged along the raised, wooden walkway over the muddy waters below. I wish I could tell you that I admired the dripping, Spanish moss hanging all over the cypresses, or stood back in awe as the walkway seemed to slip into the dark waters below, but I would be lying. I dragged my feet along the wooden ramps, complaining about the overcast day, the continuous mist, and the monster-size mosquitos that tried to penetrate the sleeves of my raincoat. I had lost my sense of humor, my sense of purpose, and slumped into the muddy waters just like the walkway did.

Here was our last national park for the year. We had traveled all around the country, and now, on our way to Florida, we ran into a roadblock, not just one roadblock, but multiple ones. If this wasn't a huge sign from the universe, I don't know what is. Having been a follower of signs for many years, I should have recognized these signs when they first appeared. After running into multiple roadblocks, I should have known that the Congaree NP wasn't open. I should have known that visiting national parks was over for me – at least for this year of 2015. Next year could be different, but this year, I was done.

With only one more day in South Carolina, it was time to move on. I was ready to leave this state without getting to see any of the beauty and charm of this Southern Belle. Perhaps, November isn't the time of year to admire the splendor of the South. November in most eastern states is a dismal, gray month, better spent on a Caribbean island than along the east coast. In any case, that was my sign from above. I had hit the end of the road, and it was time to head to Florida to escape the prediction of another snowy winter in the Northeast.

Chapter 9

RV Camping Options

Once you decide to live the Full-time RV life, there are even more choices on how to live that life on the road. In the past 10 years, the camping options have grown to fit all kinds of people from your specific interests to what you want to spend; and from the amenities that you're seeking to how you want to go about camping. There are private campgrounds, membership campgrounds, campgrounds run by RV clubs, free and cheap camping like at Wal-Mart or casinos, boondocking on the Bureau of Land Management's public lands, and the list goes on. I'm going to cover some of the favorite ways to camp, and some of the bigger RV clubs and membership clubs that are out there to choose from. It's up to you to think about your camping style. Ask yourself these questions:

- ✓ Do you like to camp out in nature, and in remote areas?
- ✓ Do you like to camp with a group of people where they have activities and lots of amenities?
- ✓ Do you like to camp with your family and pets with activities for the whole family?
- ✓ Do you like to camp at a chain of campgrounds where you know the quality and the amenities will be the same whatever state you may be camping in?
- ✓ Are you on a tight budget, and needing to find reasonably-priced campsites?

Those are some of the questions to consider as you read about the camping options available on the road today. As more Baby Boomers retire, and join the Full-time RV lifestyle, I imagine the options will increase as well. Being active retirees, they want to participate in more lively activities than bingo and shuffleboard. Perhaps, they'll be out zip lining, and hiking mountains. Here are the options.

Private campgrounds

Private campgrounds can be found in every state of the United States. Some have websites where you browse and check out sites, and even make reservations, but many will be smaller operations, and you'll still need to give them a call to reserve a site.

Many times, the private campground is the only one in the area where you're traveling so you have to take a chance. If they are part of the Good Sam Club network, then they do have to meet certain standards, and are routinely evaluated and given ratings for their services. If you're a member of the Good Sam Club, then you'll also receive a discount on the camping as well as other benefits that I'll cover in this chapter under RV clubs.

In my experience with the private campgrounds, we usually tried to look for reviews on Google, or on some of the camping apps listed in the Resource section at the end of the book. If we were only staying one night, on our way to another destination, then we'd take a chance. Sometimes, the websites of the campgrounds were deceiving. The pictures looked great, and then the reality was different, but for one night, we made it work. It's all part of the adventure of camping to try new places. Sometimes, you'll find a jewel of a campground that can really surprise you.

Franchise chain campgrounds

This type of campground reminds me of the chain hotels that you find anywhere in the country. You know what to expect when you get there, and they almost always have the same amenities. One popular franchise chain is the KOA Kampgrounds of America www.koa.com. In the past, they were known as more of a family campground, but in recent years, they have expanded and now have different types of campgrounds for different experiences from journey campgrounds which are convenient to the highway with large pull-thru sites, to holiday and resort campgrounds which offer even more activities and recreation for the whole family. They also have cabins for rent so those without a camper can join you at any KOA. Some KOAs are seasonal campgrounds opening in the spring through late fall, and closing for the winter. Of course, the KOAs in the Southern states are usually open year-round.

My husband and I liked the ease of making reservations through the KOA website, and knowing what to expect after a long day of driving. We did notice the KOAs were extremely busy in the summer months, and sometimes, the noise level was a problem when they had a family movie night which ran until 11 pm, or when your campsite happened to be near the swimming pool. If you like an active campground with similar amenities wherever you go, then the KOA choice is ideal. You can also become a KOA member to take advantage of benefits such as discounts on sites, and free nights after a certain amount of stays, but you don't have to be a member to stay at any KOA campground.

RV Clubs

As camping has become even more popular, the number of RV

clubs and associations has grown right along with the number of campers. There are clubs for all different interests and hobbies of campers from bird-watching to computers, and from kayaking to fishing. There are even clubs for clothing optional camping, but I can't personally recommend them because I haven't tried them…yet. The clubs that I am going to describe here are the bigger RV clubs that offer a host of benefits for members. The list of benefits may not include everything so check out the websites for the most up-to-date information.

Good Sam Club

The Good Sam Club www.goodsamclub.com is one of the largest RV clubs with millions of members. They offer a lot of different benefits from discounts at a network of Good Sam campgrounds, a generous discount on store items and LP gas at Camping World stores, and discounts at gas stations like Flying J and Pilot Travel Centers. They also offer additional benefits for an extra cost such as Good Sam Roadside Assistance which offers unlimited distance towing to a service area, and even covers other vehicles than your RV. For peace of mind, they also have Good Sam Travel Assist which covers some emergency medical situations along with coordinating with your family members to get you and your family home safe, and even the RV if the driver had a medical emergency.

The Good Sam Club membership has been well worth the cost, and one of the first places, we checked when looking for a campground in a new area. They listed the most campgrounds nation-wide, and it was easy to get the discount by just showing the membership card when you checked in. If you're going to purchase one RV Club membership to start, this would be the one.

Escapees RV Club

Another popular RV club is the Escapees RV Club www.escapees.com which is the go-to club for Full-Timers, mainly for all the support services that they offer including mail forwarding services for the three most popular states chosen by RVers as their domiciles – Florida, South Dakota and Texas; special services like RVers BootCamp for newbies; SmartWeigh to make sure your RV isn't tipping the scales; and Escapades, educational events and rallies held around the country. They also have Escapees Regional groups with chapters all around the country so you can meet up with RVers wherever you may be traveling. There are Escapees Special Interest Groups as well as a newer sub-group called XSCAPERS, a lifestyle group focused more on RVers who work and travel with their RV, and perhaps are younger, and, may even travel with their children.

The Escapees RV Club is another excellent one to join for the variety of services that it offers, and the special assistance for Full-timers. We stayed at a couple of their Rainbow Parks where you receive a discount as a member in Bushnell, Florida and Livingston, Texas. Both the staff and the campers were so friendly and helpful when we were newbies on the road. I haven't joined the chapters or the special interest groups because I've been busy sight-seeing and doing some work on the road. But if you'd like to have a community on the road, the Escapees would be one of the first places to check out.

Family Motor Coach Association (FMCA)

Another RV Club that is very established is the FMCA www.fmca.com They offer a comprehensive list of benefits for members from RV rallies to campground discounts, from a Medical Emergency/Travel Assistance program to Roadside

Assistance (for an extra cost.) Their benefits seem similar to the Good Sam Club so you may want to compare what works best for you. We chose Good Sam so I don't have any personal experience with this RV Club, but it does have good recommendations from other RVers that we've met on the road.

There are many other RV Clubs for more specific interests. We found Good Sam and Escapees to be the best clubs to join especially when you're new on the road. Later, you may discover that you only need one membership, or a different one more specific to your interests.

Campground Membership Clubs

Membership Clubs have also become popular around the country for RV camping. We had the pleasure of staying at a Thousand Trails RV park in Oregon because Jim had a relative who was working there. We stayed at the Mt. Hood RV Resort in Welches, Oregon during the holiday week of July 4th, and found it quite comfortable, and enjoyed all the extra amenities including a gym, swimming pool, and biking/hiking trails. They had vacation cottages for rent, and even some cottages available for purchase. The resort was just over an hour from Portland so there were many people who bought exclusive memberships for this campground so that they could visit on the week-ends all summer long. In the area around the campground, you could travel to Mt. Hood, the Columbia Gorge, and of course, Portland was not far away.

Thousand Trails and their partner, Encore RV Resorts are similar to other membership clubs where you purchase a membership to a particular campground that is part of an association of private campgrounds. The fee can be a few hundred dollars to several thousand dollars depending on how many areas you'd like to visit around the country. Some of the clubs will sell you different zones such as the Northwest, Southwest, Northeast, Southeast and Midwest where you're entitled to stay at campgrounds in that particular region, but then you would have to pay extra to go to other campgrounds in different regions.

The membership clubs seem ideal for RVers who want to explore one area of the country, or want to have the ease of staying at campgrounds that are part of a club, and similar in their quality of services. Full-time RVers usually like to do more exploring on their own first before deciding on one membership club. There are camping passes offered by Thousand Trails www.thousandtrails.com that give you unlimited camping in one zone of the country which can be a great way to spend a year exploring one region at a time. We enjoyed our one-time experience camping at a Thousand Trails campground, and maybe you would, too.

Campground Discount Clubs

Campground discount clubs provide RVers with discounts on campgrounds across the country for a membership fee. With most memberships, you can receive up to 50% off normal nightly rates at affiliated campgrounds. Campgrounds affiliate with the discount clubs because they help them fill spaces that would otherwise not get filled.

Some of the better known discount clubs are Passport America, the Happy Campers Club, and the Camp Club USA which is affiliated with Good Sam. Passport America www.passportamerica.com calls itself the original 50% discount camping club, and lists a couple thousand campgrounds on its website. We became members the first year on the road, but we had trouble finding their campgrounds that were on our travel route. When we did find some, the 50% discount only applied on certain days of the week, and times of the year.

Because we didn't want to be too restricted on when and how long we stayed at a campground, we decided to not renew our membership. If you like a deal and are willing to be flexible and follow a route that includes their campgrounds, then it might work for you.

With most of the discount clubs, it does seem that the discount only applies to off-peak times (during the week and off-season) and for limited nights. Of course, it depends on the RV Park. You have to read each RV Park's rules on the discount very carefully. We never did check out the Happy Campers Club or the Camp Club USA affiliated with the Good Sam Club. We loved using our Good Sam Club discount at many campgrounds around the country, and that worked well for us. You may want to sign up for one discount club, and give it a try. You can usually recoup the membership fee in a couple of campground visits.

RV Owners Clubs

Most RV manufacturers have RV owners clubs for those who are interested in connecting with other RVers who own an RV like their own. Some of the manufacturers even have clubs for specific RVs. If you do an internet search, you can find out the details for your specific RV and manufacturer.

Some of the clubs have membership dues, and formal rallies to meet up with other owners. Many also have blogs and forums on-line where you can share helpful information and ask questions.

We joined the Heartland RV Owners Club which was free for the first year, and then a minimal fee every year after. They host rallies once a year, but we haven't been to any of them yet. My husband has used their on-line forum to share information, and get some of his questions answered which was helpful.

We've also met up with other Bighorn owners on the road, and it was fun to give and receive helpful information. The RV owners club is another way to connect with other RVers, and some of the rallies are quite formal, even offering service appointments during the time of the rally. They are certainly worth checking out, and could lead to making some new friends who share the love of RVing in the same RV as you.

Public Campgrounds in State Parks and National Parks

Most state parks and national parks have their own campgrounds. Some are quite large, and others on a smaller scale. When it comes to the state parks, they are usually found on the websites for the individual states. The state campgrounds also have limited hook-ups, and almost always no internet or cable TV hook-ups. The rules also vary about making reservations, and how long you can stay each time.

Emigrant Lake RV Park, one of the state parks in Ashland, Oregon

The national park campgrounds require more advance planning. If you know you want to stay at Yellowstone NP in June, then you probably want to book as far ahead as you can, maybe even a year ahead. Some of the NP campgrounds are also not that suitable for the larger RVs because they were designed when most people camped in smaller RVs, and tents. We never camped within the NPs, but we usually found plenty of private campgrounds in the vicinity of a NP. Within the NPs, I was always amazed to see large Class A Mobile Homes touring the park with their whole rig even including the towed car. I'm not sure why they didn't just park their rig outside the park and unhitch the tow vehicle to drive around in. Some RVers seem to enjoy a challenge.

In our travels in the state park systems, we stayed at the Emigrant Lake RV Park in Ashland, Oregon which was a state park on a lake with large sites, and an on-line reservation system through the Jackson County Parks Office. The site overlooked the lake, and it really had a spacious feeling. Of course, we were there in June before the summer rush, but off-season, it was a relaxing and beautiful place to stay, close to Ashland, a cultural city with the well-known Oregon Shakespeare Theatre which made the time there even more memorable.

Lake Erie State Park in Brocton, New York

Another state park was the Lake Erie State Park in Brocton, New York where we stayed twice, once in August when it was very, busy on a week-end, and the second time a year later, in September, a lot nicer and quieter, and we booked the best site in the campground overlooking the lake. The park has lots of green grass, and trees which can make it challenging for bigger rigs. We had to back into our campsite both times, and the overhanging trees can make it a challenge for a newbie. They also only have electric hook-ups so you have to fill your water tank on the way in, and dump your gray and black water tanks on the way out. Even with less hook-ups, it is still a beautiful campground near the vineyards of upstate New York, and one of the closest campgrounds to Lily Dale, a Spiritualist summer camp.

For the Lake Erie State Park, we made reservations through www.reserveamerica.com which is the website that handles several state park systems as well as federal campgrounds. Most of the time, you're making the reservations on-line so if you need to talk to a person, they don't always know a lot about the individual campgrounds. In hindsight, I think I would see if I knew anyone who lives in the state that I am traveling through, and see if they know of a state park that they enjoy in their home state. Most people have a favorite park that they love to visit, and that's probably your best recommendation.

As far as federal campgrounds and Corps of Engineers (COE) campgrounds, you can do a map search on www.recreation.gov to find a campground on your travel route. Some of the federal campgrounds you can reserve sites, but many are first come, first serve. Some other websites to check out for more federal camping options are: the National Park Service at www.nps.gov/findapark/index.htm, the National Forest Service at www.fs.fed.us/recreation/map/finder.shtml, and Bureau of Land Management's (BLM) home page at www.blm.gov/wo/st/en.html where you can click on a state to get to that state's BLM page. A private website featuring

National Forest Campgrounds is at www.forestcamping.com.

Many of these camping options are more remote, and off the beaten path so you want to plan your travel route accordingly. Check out the route on Google Maps, and on your personal GPS to see if you can drive your big rig there. Some RVers are more adventurous, and will take their rigs into these remote areas to have the camping experience of being off the grid which is what the next section is about called boondocking.

Boondocking (also known as Dry Camping and Wild Camping)

Some Full-time RVers love to boondock, and spend most of their time, living off the grid. Boondocking is camping without hook-ups where you have to rely on the on-board systems of your RV. It is certainly more of a true camping experience, spending time in nature, and getting to see some unspoiled areas of this great country. As I mentioned in the previous section, the Bureau of Land Management's (BLM) home page is www.blm.gov/wo/st/en.html. When you go to their website, you can click on a state to get to the state BLM page where you can find some of the prime places for wild camping. The National Forest campgrounds can also be places to have a boondocking experience.

It's probably wise to try out boondocking not too far from civilization to see how you enjoy it. There are even rallies around boondocking that educate newbies to the lifestyle. The price is certainly right, almost always free.

Once you get hooked on the wild camping experience, the big investment seems to be buying the solar panels, an inverter, and a battery bank so that you can last longer without electricity. Most RVs have their own batteries that generate some power for times when you are camping without electricity. You can usually last a couple of days, but you're unable to use big household appliances such as your microwave and television. To run big appliances, you could run a generator, which would also re-charge your batteries. With the generator, you do have the noise factor as well as needing to bring along extra gas/propane.

With boondocking, you also need to pay attention to water conservation because you need to fill up your fresh water tanks for showers and sometimes drinking water unless you carry large plastic bottles just for your water. Then, while, you're dry camping, you have to watch your water use – limiting the length of your showers, and how you wash dishes. Once you head back to civilization, then you'd need to find a dump station which are at most public and private campgrounds as well as truck stops.

Propane becomes even more important in wild camping. Your household appliances including your refrigerator and water heater are able to run on propane when electricity isn't available. Of course, you may also need the propane for heat when the temperatures drop at night in the desert or mountain areas. Some RVers even enjoy a bit of winter boondocking, but I imagine that is an acquired taste.

With wild camping, you may also have to upgrade your mobile hot spot on your smart phone for phone and internet use. The major phone/internet providers could give you some suggestions as well, but then you may also want to really get away from it all including your phone, internet and television.

My husband and I haven't personally tried boondocking other than at a Wal-Mart parking lot, but we have seen other RVers in some amazingly beautiful places out in nature. In Southern California in the Alabama Hills near the town of Lone Pine, we spied some Fifth Wheels camping right in the middle of the red rocks and rolling hills where many westerns were filmed. You could just picture John Wayne riding through those hills on his horse. In Lone Pine, they even have a film history museum dedicated to the films that took place in those famous Alabama Hills. Boondocking in the Alabama Hills looked like a great place to make a movie of your own.

Alabama Hills in Lone Pine, California

Free and Low-cost Camping

Most people have seen or heard of RVers camping in Wal-Mart parking lots, and that is one way to travel cheaply when you're driving cross-country. Flying J truck stops are also open to RVs camping for a night. Most of the parking lot camping experiences are fine for one night. It's always wise to check with the Wal-Mart store manager to make sure they still accept overnight RV guests because some Wal-Marts don't. It also makes sense to do some shopping and dining there to support the business that's giving you that free campsite. Be respectful as well, and don't open all your awnings, and start setting up your lawn chairs and grill. It's still their parking lot, and they may ask you to leave at that point. You don't want to spoil the "Free" benefit for everyone else.

A helpful website is www.freecampgrounds.com. The site does not provide campground listings, but it includes links to free

RV campsite resources as well as helpful tips for boondockers. The website also offers a useful list of Wal-Marts that do not permit overnight RV parking.

Casinos are another option for reasonably-priced campgrounds. Some of the casinos have RV parks with hook-ups, and others allow you to park overnight for free in their parking lots. In the west, I stayed at a casino campground with full hook-ups for $10 a night in an enclosed area right near the front entrance of the casino. It was a positive experience, and fun to have some different entertainment while making a cross-country trip. A good resource is the www.casinocamper.com to look for RV-friendly casinos. You can search listings by state to find casinos that allow overnight RV parking. RV campers have also contributed information to this website and have given their personal opinions on every aspect of casino camping, from safety to amenities. If you enjoy gambling, it's a win-win situation.

US military RV parks are also less expensive places to camp for active duty members, military retirees and their immediate families. Many also accommodate reservists, National Guard members and Department of Defense civilian employees. The campsites can range between $10 and $30 per day. Many military campgrounds require advance reservations. The Army's Paths Across America www.armymwr.com list details under Outdoor Recreation for each campground and provide links to the websites of military bases with RV pads. Since most military campgrounds are on base, you'll need your military ID card, vehicle registration and proof of insurance to use.

Jim and I have done some Wal-Mart, and casino camping, mainly for the experience. The Wal-Mart experience isn't for everyone, but in our first year, we tried it three times for good measure. I was impressed with the number of rigs at some

Wal-Marts, and how luxurious some of the RVs were. I guess everyone likes a deal. It's also something to write home about. And that's what I've done at the end of this chapter.

Moochdocking (Last, but not least)

This is how many Full-time RVers camp the first time out. Once, you've sold your home, and there's no going back, you may end up camping in a relative or friend's driveway or yard. This is how many get used to their new RV home before heading out on the road. The official word for this camping option is Moochdocking for obvious reasons. Full-time RVers often do this as they travel around the country, visiting family and friends. It's always wise to not stay too long, or overstep your boundaries because then you may never be invited back again. In all cases, bring a gift, and enjoy some time with family and friends before you head out on the open highway once again.

Finding your Camping Style

Choosing a campground and selecting where you want to camp are very personal choices. Some Full-time RVers love to go boondocking out in wild and remote areas, getting way off the grid. Others love to camp with a group of people, always returning to a favorite campground like in an Escapees or KOA campground. Some love a deal and seek out the free and cheaper campgrounds, staying at Wal-Marts and casinos along the way. Those who still enjoy working from time to time will look for the workamping and/or volunteering opportunities at campgrounds and plan their route accordingly.

After traveling for a year, most RVers discover their own camping style. I would suggest trying some if not all of the camping options. You'll get a feel for what you like and enjoy in a campground. More often than not, this will change as you gain experience.

Our Camping Style

In our first year of camping, we made a huge circle around the country focused on seeing national parks, and also visiting family and friends along the way. We stayed in all kinds of campgrounds, from private to state, from natural settings to roadside campgrounds, from Wal-Marts to casinos, and from luxury campgrounds to a campground in a parking lot. After that year, we learned a lot about what we liked in a campground, and what we didn't like as much.

Our favorite campgrounds are out in nature with great views of a mountain, lake, river or ocean. And yet, we also like campgrounds that are convenient to major highways. Hauling a 39 foot Fifth Wheel with a large truck, we didn't always feel like driving for miles on winding roads to get to a remote campground. At times, we're happy to camp near a busy area, and leave the RV at the campground, and go off sight-seeing.

We discovered that after camping in some very, small towns that we also enjoyed camping near busier areas from time to time where shopping and dining out are more convenient. It seems that a balance of both works best for us.

As far as the campsite, the more spacious the better. We stayed in some "awning to awning" parks where your neighbor's RV was over-looking your picnic table and outdoor area. At those parks, I didn't feel as comfortable sitting outside, and having dinner or just relaxing outdoors at my campsite. Since my husband began workamping, we have been given some wonderful sites in those campgrounds. I don't know, but maybe, the campground owners were so happy to have some reliable help that they wanted us to have a great site. I am sure that doesn't happen every time, but it does seem to be a nice bonus. I'll write more about workamping in Chapter 10.

When it comes to hook-ups, we do tend to look for full hook-ups which usually include electric, water, and sewer. The extras - Wi-Fi and cable are always nice, but cable hasn't been something we've needed since we travel with a satellite for television. We also have the mobile hotspots in our T-Mobile phones so we can manage without the Wi-Fi at the campground as well. We have stayed at some scenic state parks that were worth the stay even though they had minimal hook-ups. If you're able to live without the hook-ups because you have solar panels, a battery bank, and/or generator; and you're willing to fill up your water tanks, and dump later after your camping trip, then your camping options do increase.

In our time on the road, we haven't used the swimming pools and game rooms at campgrounds that often, but have used laundry facilities all the time, and on-site gyms occasionally. Of course, those are personal preferences. Some RVers enjoy the swimming pools and hot tubs, and special activities such as movie nights, family events, and even playgrounds for pets.

One of our biggest pet peeves was that most campgrounds don't recycle. If they do, it's only aluminum cans like soda and beer cans where they cash them in for the deposit. I hope more campgrounds will catch up soon, and begin more recycling programs. In the meantime, we have taken our recycled items to national and sometimes state parks. At least, we were able to recycle some of the time.

In the future, I think I would try some boondocking in remote areas, but I'm not quite ready to invest in the extras like solar panels and batteries. I would just bring along a generator.

We have stayed at some noisy campgrounds that either had train tracks nearby, or airports or even major highways. Many campgrounds seem to be built in areas near highways especially for convenience, but also near train tracks and airports, probably because the land was cheaper for them to purchase. Since most people don't stay at campgrounds long-term, they usually put up with some noise if it's only for one night or even a week. But if you're doing seasonal camping in one location for a while, you may want to check with the campground manager about the location, and what's around it before making your reservation.

Jim has even used Google Earth to get a closer look at a possible campground. That way, you can see the terrain around the campground, and even how spaced apart the campsites are. We've also called campground managers, and some have even down-played the noise level of their campground, and then when we arrived it was a very different experience. Some of the RV parks are also not great about enforcing the rules around pets, quiet hours, and the maintenance of RVs that seem to be more permanently located in the campground. That's where checking on-line reviews is helpful.

If you're going to stay at a new campground, I would suggest checking out the reviews on Google, and also a great website at www.RVParkReviews.com. There are also some good apps for reviewing sites – one that Jim likes is RVparky. And now, for my free camping experiences at Wal-Mart.

Another Camping Adventure - Camping at Wal-Mart

Camping out in a Wal-Mart parking lot is an experience not to be missed. Jim and I stayed at three Wal-Marts during our first year around the country, but the third night ended our time at Wal-Marts – at least for 2015.

Before heading out on the road, many people had told us about staying for free in Wal-Mart parking lots. They mentioned that if you ever got stuck on the road without a campground reservation that camping at a Wal-Mart is always an option.

Our first trip down the east coast with the Bighorn RV, Jim and I stayed in our first Wal-Mart parking lot in Walterboro, South Carolina. After two nights in hotels in the northern states because of the cold December weather, we camped our first night in the RV in a Wal-Mart parking lot. We showed up late in the day, and there were already about five campers in the parking lot off to the side. Jim followed the way they had lined up in the parking lot, and chose a spot in the middle. By nightfall, we were surrounded by RVs on all sides. The flock of snowbirds had caught up with us as we made our way to Florida. There were Minnie Winnies, silver Airstreams and luxurious Class A motor homes with on-board generators so they could watch their big screen TVs even in a Wal-Mart parking lot.

We stayed in our second Wal-Mart in Stuart, Florida near where our Bighorn RV had some service done. Jim had made a reservation for a campground, but it was further north, and too late to get there when the RV had to stay in the shop until closing time. Luckily, the RV shop recommended this Wal-Mart often to campers. As dusk settled over the palm trees, we pulled in next to a couple of campers out by the edge of the parking lot. In this Wal-Mart experience, the other campers were a friendly bunch, and curious about our trip. Jim chatted with them about their experiences on the road which mostly included looking for the best fishing spots in Florida.

The next morning, we packed up, and headed to Bushnell in northern Florida which turned out to be our country experience in Florida, and not at all what I expected to find in this state. After a week there, we drove along the panhandle of Florida towards Louisiana to get to New Orleans in time for the Mardi Gras celebrations.

Our final stay at a Wal-Mart parking lot took place in Tallahassee, Florida. We actually checked out two Wal-Mart parking lots which tells you a lot about the area. Tallahassee was more of a city experience, and a lot bigger than I had imagined. The first parking lot turned out to be really small, and turning the camper around was a major project. A car camper started beeping his horn madly when Jim got close to the front end of his car. That was enough to make up our minds to find another Wal-Mart. Not too far away, another Wal-Mart showed up on the GPS. When we arrived there, I was overjoyed to see a larger parking lot, but there were also no other campers around. Jim chose a prime spot close to a wall, under some lights and not too far from the entrance. We waited for other campers to show up.

As night settled in, we kept peeking outside, and no other campers ever arrived. I wondered if other RVers knew something that we didn't know about this area. We also had parked in a part of the parking lot where people cut through from one plaza to another. We'd hear cars zooming by, but no one ever stopped. All night, Jim and I kept vigil, imagining our own personal nightmares of what could go wrong in a Wal-Mart parking lot in the middle of the night.

That's when it dawned on me, that we each have our own personal sense of security. If I felt secure in the space around me, I was fine sleeping inside my Bighorn RV. But knowing that my RV was parked in a precarious position in a Wal-Mart parking lot did not give me a sense of inner peace. I felt like I was on guard all night, wondering who was driving and/or walking by my rig, and of course, imagining the worst. After that experience, I gave up camping at Wal-Mart for that year. Now that enough time has passed and I have been camping all over this country, I think I would give it another try. But I would be very selective about where the Wal-Mart is located, preferring more country locations. I think casino parking lots might also be a better option – a lot better food, and entertainment unless you prefer people-watching at Wal-Mart. It all depends on your taste for free or cheap camping experiences.

Chapter 10

Working and Volunteering on the Road

Most Full-time RVers begin the journey, exploring the country and enjoying the freedom of their new lifestyle. After about six months, you usually have a better idea of what your monthly expenses are living on the road, and you may start to think about making some extra money to cover some of those expenses. Workamping is one of your best options for reducing your monthly expenses.

Workamping, a phrase coined by *Workamper News* (WN) is receiving money or other benefits in exchange for services performed while living in your RV. Many of these workamper positions in WN are at campgrounds and resorts, so in exchange for your work, you often receive a free campsite which includes the full hook-ups (sometimes a set amount on the electric usage); free or discounted propane; free or discounted laundry; free internet (if they have it); free cable TV (if they have it); discounts in their store (if they have one); and sometimes, free local phone service. If they don't provide these extra benefits, then there is usually some monetary compensation.

Workamper News www.workamper.com is one of the main sources for matching RVers with jobs around the country. By becoming a member, you then receive job announcements through their on-line bi-monthly magazine, and also daily emails if you prefer. The jobs at campgrounds range from camp hosts running the campground to office staff; from maintenance work to landscaping; and of course the favorite, cleaning bathrooms. The hours and wages of the jobs vary. Most employers expect 15 - 20 hours a week of work in exchange for the free campsite, but if you're willing to work more hours, then they usually pay you for the additional hours. Most of the time, the pay is close to minimum wage for the state that you're working in. Sometimes, for more skilled labor such as construction, electrical or other specialized skills, then they will pay a higher hourly wage. There are also many other kinds of jobs listed in Workamper News.

Another good website for jobs around the country is www.CoolWorks.com. They are not just for RVers, but they do advertise many positions that include RV sites as well as concessionaires that hire employees in national parks and other desirable locations.

The workamper jobs are often seasonal such as for the summer, from May to September, or for the winter season in the southern states which is often from November to April. Some campgrounds are more flexible, hiring workampers for only a month at a time, but the longer the commitment such as four months or longer, then there is often a bonus paid at the end of the season.

There are also shorter workamper jobs like around Christmas or other holiday sales periods (such as Christmas tree sales, pumpkin sales, fireworks sales, kiosks in malls during Christmas, Amazon.com holiday shipping season, etc.). These jobs may last only a month or six to eight weeks, but they also have very intense work schedules.

Some RVers also choose to do volunteer work instead, receiving the free campsite for their volunteering, but not always having to make the same commitment as a "paid" workamper. This is also another way to cut down your monthly expenses, and also give back by volunteering at state parks, national parks and wildlife refuges. Some people prefer volunteering because they feel freer to leave if they need to, and also they don't have to deal with the tax implications for paid work.

The biggest benefit of workamping or volunteering is that you're lowering your monthly expenses. When my husband workamps, our monthly expenses have been cut in half. Of course, that's also because we're not spending as much money on sight-seeing and driving around. When you're staying in one place for three months or longer, then you're spending less on the driving of the RV. After you've seen the major sights in the area, you may also just enjoy spending time in nature which is almost always free.

My husband's first workamping experience was as a Camp Host where he worked an average of 60 hours over a five-day work week from May through Labor Day, and handled all kinds of duties from guiding people to their campsites to lawn care/maintenance; and from enforcing the campground rules to handling emergencies in the middle of the night. He did receive a free campsite, and monetary compensation each month for filling propane tanks, and handling his duties. After he completed the four months, he also received a bonus. Finding the job through *Workamper News*, Jim interviewed over the phone, and signed a contract. His thoughts after the experience were that he learned a lot about the running of a campground, and handling all kinds of situations. In the future though, he decided the 60 plus hours a week commitment even with the extra pay was more than he wanted to take on. Since that experience, he decided he'd rather do 20 hours a week for a free campsite, with possible overtime, but not committed to doing more than 20 hours a week. Jim now prefers an hourly "handyman" position rather than a "salaried" Camp Host position.

His second workamping experience was more in alignment with those preferences. Jim was hired to only do special projects/maintenance at a campground where he utilized his carpentry skills and other handyman skills. The workamping job was also in the off-season for four months so it was nice and quiet. We had a prime site with lots of space, and a great lake view. The campground owner was very generous so along with a free campsite, we also had free propane, free laundry, free electricity, a store discount, and occasional lunches along with sight-seeing passes. Jim also received a higher hourly wage for work over 20 hours a week, and a bonus at the end of the four month period. For this job, he also interviewed over the phone, and signed a contract before arriving which had the contingency that either party could end the agreement at any time.

Both workamping jobs were positive learning experiences, but like finding the perfect campground, it seems that over time, you would get a better idea of what kind of workamper position is right for you. And that may be a volunteer position depending on your financial needs.

Workamping and volunteering are definitely making it easier for people to live the Full-time RV lifestyle without it costing as much. Both options allow you to save money, and have the pleasure of exploring one area for a longer period of time. Some people prefer more freedom especially moving around more in the first year, but after a year or two, workamping may be an option that you'd like to pursue. If you're younger than 65, it does help to have more than one source of income. Workamping can be one source along with your investments, and hobbies that you may turn into a business. On the road, I've continued to do some counseling work, and writing. On-line businesses are great for the road as long as you have a secure internet connection. Time for another tale about the location of Jim's first workamping job in Utah.

A Workamping Adventure – Diversity on the Road

After a year and a half on the road, Jim decided to take on his first workamping job. After a couple of phone interviews, Jim had his first summer job on the road as a Camp Host for the Holiday Hills RV Park in Coalville, Utah. It was a small campground, only 42 campsites alongside the Weber River which fed into nearby Echo Lake. The campground was surrounded by rocky, red hills where cattle and horses roamed within sight of the cross-country Highway 80.

Arriving there the end of April, I planned on working on a travel memoir for the summer. Right away, I was struck by the contrast of the surrounding communities. The town of Coalville was tiny compared to the larger surrounding cities of Salt Lake City and Park City. The downtown of Coalville consisted of one Main Street with storefronts, and homes from the turn of the century. I strolled into the Summit Furniture and Mercantile Company, the local general store which was built in 1908, and still run by the same family. The hardwood floorboards creaked under my feet as I marveled at all the items for sale from groceries to Levi jeans; from Mother's Day cards to cowboy hats. The store included a small butcher shop as well as a selection of hardware items. It truly was a general store. In town, there were a couple of family restaurants, and the only chain restaurant that I noticed was Subway.

After my trip to downtown Coalville, I decided to explore the nearest big city of Park City, Utah where the Winter Olympics in 2002 took place. Under the still snow-covered mountains, I entered a whole other world. Talk about culture shock. Driving over from my campground, I stepped into a world that reminded me of the San Francisco Bay area.

I stopped at one Starbucks to get a coffee, and experienced the afternoon coffee rush hour. There were students, mothers with young children, and working people all lined up. I commented to one young mother about the long line, and she told me that it was always like this in the afternoon – the time in between school being let out, and before all the after-school activities had begun. She then proceeded to ask her two young children what they wanted for their afternoon snack. They both got chocolate milks, and then a banana muffin, and a chocolate croissant. Along with her personal coffee order, I think I heard the Starbucks barista tell her the order total was $20 something. The young mother then began socializing with all the other mothers who were also waiting in line for their re-fueling for the second half of their day.

After my quiet life in Coalville, I felt like I already had a caffeine buzz even before I sipped my iced mocha. I was in awe of all the activity, and thought I had been thrust back into one of my "past lives" living in the Bay area. Then I headed to Whole Foods, not a store that I've seen too often on my trip around the country. Again, I was overwhelmed by all the activity, and the abundance of healthy choices. Luckily, I had a shopping list, but I still ended up piling some extra goodies into my shopping cart. Most people have joked about Whole Foods, and how it takes your whole paycheck to shop there. I knew I wouldn't be coming here too often for my groceries, but for only special treats, and healthy alternatives not found anywhere else.

After noticing more stores that reminded me of my days living in California, I headed back to my small town life in Coalville. Still reeling from the culture shock, I couldn't believe that Park City was only 25 minutes away from my campground. Even though the two towns were that close, they were like night and day.

The experience made me wonder how different groups of people can live only a few exits apart on the highway. And yet, one lifestyle seemed to be more affluent, and focused on material consumption; and the other lifestyle, more centered on maintaining a small town atmosphere with friendliness and a slower pace of life.

I am not judging either lifestyle because I've lived in both kinds of places. I know the incredible benefits that I gained from living in the San Francisco Bay area, and also know the amazing riches that I experienced, living in the Gold Country of California. Both places were incredible learning experiences for me, and both shaped and molded who I am today.

I love the diversity of experiences in this great country of the United States, and continue to marvel at all that I've seen on my trip around the country.

Jim as the Camp Host with Denise & Jacob Fisher

Chapter 11

Mishaps and Adventures of RV Life

The life of the Full-time RVer doesn't always go smoothly. There will be break-downs, mishaps and adventures on the road. Once you realize that every RV owner goes through these times, then it's a bit less stressful even though it can throw a wrench in your plans. Of course, the more you keep up with the maintenance and service of your RV along with utilizing some of those safety tools in Chapter 6 on RV Safety, then you can minimize some of the events.

If you do have to take your RV to the shop for repairs at a dealership or a service center, always check to see if the repairs are covered by your manufacturer's warranty or under an extended warranty. It's best to address the warranty as soon as you schedule the appointment.

When it comes to working with a RV dealer or service center, some won't work on an RV that wasn't purchased at their site, but many will. Full-time RVers and those who are stranded far from home are usually taken care of first before the locals who might not need service right away. It does help to be flexible and friendly, and maybe, even give them something extra like homemade goodies. Before I knew about these niceties, at one of our service appointments, I gave the crew some ice cream that was only going to melt in our RV. They were appreciative, and maybe, it did make a difference in the work that they did.

Campground Mishaps

When Jim was a Camp Host in Utah, he saw many mishaps at the campground. Some could have been prevented if campers took the time to check out the area around their campsite before parking their RV or taking off without checking out the exit road. Some RVers will walk the route to their campsite from the office where they check in, just to see the route, and if there are any potential hazards like low-hanging branches, power poles, fences, etc. Getting safely to your campsite is always easier in the daylight, but sometimes, you will have to arrive after dark, making it even more important that you check out the route to your site. Many times, after hours, you'll pick up your campsite # and a package at the closed campground office, and then you'll have to find your way to the site. Easier said, then done, but take your time, and get to your site safely.

Being a Camp Host, Jim also had to deal with some medical emergencies at the campground. It's not easy to think about emergencies when you're planning the trip of a lifetime, but it's important to be prepared. An important must: To have health insurance that can cover all or at least part of the medical emergencies that happen outside of your home state. To be extra prepared, you could sign up for one of the plans offered by RV Clubs that can give you some extra coverage such as the Good Sam Travel Assist Program or the FMCA's Medical Emergency/Travel Assistance program. Both programs are listed in Chapter 9 under RV Clubs. Even if you never have to use them, they will give you some peace of mind on the road.

Other more minor issues are awning incidents unless you have to replace an awning, and then it can become a major issue. At first, in Florida, we used to leave out the awning on our RV, and tied it to a sunscreen as well as anchored to the ground. But the wind would often come up at night, and then we'd have to go outside and undo the awning and the sunscreen. It became a hassle so we went back to putting out the awning by itself when we needed some sun or light rain protection. When you leave out the awning to protect you from rain, make sure it's angled on one side so the awning can drain the water to that side. That way, in a heavy downpour, your awning won't fill up with water, and then the weight of the water can rip it off your RV. It's wise to never leave your awning out when you leave the RV for a while. In many parts of the country, there are gusty winds, and the wind can tear the awning right off your RV - not a cheap item to replace. The strong winds can also blow away all kinds of items including your outdoor carpets/mats, chairs, plants, etc. If you're going to be away all day, it's probably wise to put away some of those items, or at least, place some heavy rocks on top of them.

Winter RVing Adventures

Winter RVing at Rutledge Lake RV Resort near Asheville, NC

Most RVers only experience three seasons of the year - spring, summer and fall - because most either avoid winter in the northern states, or head south for the winter. When you become a Full-time RVer, you can encounter some cold winter weather once and a while, or more often, depending where you head for the winter months. In the first year of RVing, Jim and

I made a big circle around the country so we only spent a couple of months in Florida before beginning our drive to the Mardi Gras celebrations in February in New Orleans – that's where we first got to experience some colder weather. As the temperatures dropped, we relied more on our fireplace heater as well as the RV furnace that ran on propane. Even with the Artic package, our Bighorn RV became cold quickly once the temperatures plummeted. As we drove further west, we ran into snow in New Mexico. It was only a dusting, but enough to make us realize that RVing in the winter can be a whole new experience. Now, you have to keep an eye on your propane supply because you don't want to be running out of fuel in the middle of the night.

Some RVers invest in RV skirting which is made out of different materials, and comes in panels that are then attached to the bottom of the RV. These skirts can make a big difference in the colder and windy states. They save on electricity/propane, and keep your rig a lot warmer in the winter months even preventing frozen pipes and tanks in most climates. The skirts work great if you're staying in one place for a while. Even though we spent a colder winter in one location, we didn't invest in the RV skirt because the temperatures went up and down often. If we had wintered in Colorado, Minnesota or even, our home state of South Dakota, we would definitely get an RV skirt. You can make your own skirt from simple Styrofoam boards, plywood panels, or from polyester reinforced vinyl panels; or buy a custom-made skirt just for your RV. Of course, the cost varies, but if you're going to spend winter in the colder climates, then it may be worth it to invest in a skirt. Going skirt-less in the winter could be a costly adventure in more ways than one.

Another great item for the colder climates is a heated water hose that you plug in, keeping the water hose that goes into your RV warm on those cold nights. That makes a big difference especially when the temps drop into the single digits. Another handy item has been a small electric heater, not just for heating your feet, but for heating under the RV to keep your water tanks from freezing. It's something you also learn by doing. After a couple of very, cold nights, Jim discovered that our gray and black water tanks were frozen. Basically, he went to drain them, and that's how he discovered it. He joked, "I think we have a poopsicle." After getting the portable electric heater out, he turned it on, and placed it in a location where it blew hot air into the basement of the RV near the tanks. Slowly, the tanks warmed up, and later that day, he was able to drain them.

Winter RVing is not necessarily for newbies, but you can learn some new survival skills. My suggestions are just the tip of the iceberg (pardon the pun) because Jim and I have had only brief winter experiences in New England, in the Southwest and in Asheville, North Carolina. We've had enough experiences with winter in those locations to know that going further north in our RV in the winter is not something we'll be doing on a regular basis. But, we can claim, "We've survived winter in an RV without frozen pipes, and only a couple of frozen tanks." Live and learn.

Animal Adventures

Camping outdoors can give you a new appreciation for wildlife of all kinds. When you're living in your RV home Full-time, you may have to deal with a few invasions of animals, just like in your former traditional home. There can be ants, spiders, mice, snakes, and some critters which you've never seen before in your life. Some of these critters will be poisonous. I don't want to alarm you, but it's a good idea to check out what kinds of animals are in the state that you're visiting so that you can be more aware when they show up.

Having lived in California for 17 years, I had seen my share of rattlesnakes, hiking in the foothills and mountains near where I lived. I also kept a look out for black widow and brown recluse spiders. All of these critters have crossed my path more than once, and even lived around my house. Most of the time, I was more worried about one of my cats having an encounter with one of these animals.

Of course, there are bigger animals that you may see on your adventures around the country such as bear, moose, elk, alligators/crocodiles, buffalo, mountain lions, bobcats etc. In all of my travels, I've only seen those kinds of animals from a distance. I've never been surprised by one on a hiking trail, or at my campsite, but I am well aware that can happen. So when Jim and I do go hiking out in the woods, we bring along some bear spray, and a small first aid kit. Depending on the length of the excursion, we sometimes bring along more emergency supplies, but we only go on day hikes so we bring what we feel is necessary. In the Resource section at the end of the book, there is a list of our suggested hiking supplies.

Even with all the planning, you never know when you'll have a personal encounter with some wildlife. My encounter came in Oregon in a campground. This was even after I had been warned about the bug life there. I guess I thought I was immune, but it certainly became one of my more eventful nights on the road. Let's just say, I should have Zigged when I Zagged.

A Wildlife Adventure – Zapped by a Bug near Zig Zag, Oregon

My first trip ever into Portland turned out to be one of the hottest days of the summer. Expecting cool breezes from this environmentally green city, I almost wilted under a hot July sun. Dressed for a day in the gardens, I wore a purple flower dress topped with a wide-brimmed white hat. Jim and I planned on visiting the Rose Gardens and the Japanese Gardens that have made Portland famous. Driving around the downtown into a residential area known as Washington Park, we discovered the gardens in the early afternoon. The roses blossomed everywhere, but they even drooped under the heat, spilling their petals along the brick paths. Tourists huddled under the shady arbors of roses, bypassing the paths out in the sizzling sun.

After an hour or so in the rose gardens, Jim and I crossed the street to venture into the shady Japanese gardens. With the flowing rivers and inviting pools of water, the Japanese gardens were still quite warm, but all the water gave the illusion of coolness. Sitting on a bench near a dark pool of water framed by purple irises, I breathed in the quiet serenity of the garden. Walking along a wooden zig zag path, I spied goldfish of brilliant orange and pale ivory gliding below in and out of the bamboo reeds. One rocky path led down a hill to benches tucked into the towering bamboo with a wooden tub fountain trickling water. Sitting in such tranquility was more inviting than walking in the steamy heat. Eventually, hunger pains inspired me to leave the cool greenness in search of food.

Jim and I thought there would be more restaurants around

the gardens, but we only found a snack shack, offering simple treats of ice cream, cool drinks, and sweets. We walked down the hill through a residential neighborhood of elegant homes with fancy fences and flowering shrubs. Not getting any closer to town, we hopped a shuttle back to Washington Park where our truck was parked, and then drove into town. The items in a natural foods store looked tempting, but I needed something more substantial. Hot pizza didn't sound appealing after walking on the steaming sidewalks. Then, rounding the corner, I spied the Elephants Delicatessen, but this was no ordinary deli. This deli had marble countertops with cake dishes and silver trays with pastries and cookies. Gleaming glass cases displayed all kinds of salads, deli meats, and loaves of bread. They even had a coffee and wine bar. Overwhelmed by the delectable choices, I only chose a cool green salad, and a sweet iced tea while Jim ordered one of his favorites – a tuna melt sandwich.

Eventually, I cooled down enough to put on a light sweater. Tempted by the coffee bar, I ordered a latte which the barista served in a white ceramic cup topped with froth in the design of a feather. Sipping my coffee, I imagined living in this neighborhood, visiting this deli every week. Many people came in by themselves, selecting solitary tables. They all seemed to know the wait staff. Leaving behind their hot city apartments for a refreshing break at their corner deli, I envied their proximity to such a delightful establishment. After finishing my latte, it was time to head back to the campground near the town of Zig Zag, Oregon. I liked the name, pondering using it as a title for a book, something like *Zig Zagging with Zeus around the Country*.

Once I got back to the camper, Zeus paced at the door, anxious for a walk. After a quiet day by himself, he was ready to venture out, and explore the neighborhood. Most of the time, he didn't go too far, snooping around the neighbors' campsites. In this campground, there were also cabins that people rented for their summer vacations or week-end retreats. On both sides of our RV, tiny home cabins tempted Zeus to sniff around them. After exploring the bushes and gardens around the cabins, he headed out to the street. Dusk settled into the tops of the evergreen trees. With enough light, I allowed Zeus to explore even further. We walked by a log cabin with a For Sale sign. I walked closer to read the cabin's name, "Raven's Rest."

Right at that moment, a flying bug dove down from a tree, stabbing my left hand, right in the vein. I yelled out, "Get off!" yanking the bug off my hand.

Jim came running over, "What happened?"

"A bug stabbed me like a needle!" I looked down at my hand which was already turning red. Jim handed me his cold can of beer. I placed it on my throbbing hand, walking back to the RV.

Jim's cousin worked at the campground with her husband, selling campground memberships. She had warned me about the bugs in Oregon, and how vicious they could be. I thought that maybe she was exaggerating the tales of deadly bugs, but not after that encounter. Jim called her up, and she brought over some remedies, an anti-itch cream and some medication for the allergic reaction. I texted my friend, Gloria for essential oil suggestions, and she mentioned purification and lavender oils so I applied both of those.

With my hand swelling up, I peeled off my sticky clothes after the hot day to take a shower. I thought that might make me feel better. Afterwards, I felt cleaner, but my hand still throbbed. I sat down in the recliner, ready to enjoy a snack of milk and cookies. As I sat there, I started to feel hotter and hotter. I pressed my hand to my chest, feeling a tightness near my heart. I found it harder to breath, and thought I might pass out. I didn't think I was having a heart attack, but some reaction to this bug bite. With my hand now ballooned out, I could see what it would look like if I gained 60 pounds. My right hand was still thin with the raised, blue veins, but my left hand was pudgy with no wrinkles at all. I hesitated to speak.

"Jim, I'm not feeling too well. Maybe, I need to go to the hospital."

Jim sat up right away. "You want me to take you there, Now?"

"I'm afraid if I stand up that I might pass out. Better call 911."

Now, Jim stood up. "Are you sure? It's that bad?"

I leaned back further into the chair. "I don't know. I've never felt this way after a bug bite."

Jim grabbed his cell phone, not hesitating any longer, and called 911.

In the now, dark campground, the firetruck drove in without its flashing lights. A couple of EMTs barely in their 20's rapped on the door of the RV with their supervisor following behind. Jim guided them in to where I rested on the recliner. They peppered me with questions while checking my vitals. I showed them my hand, and they asked about the mystery bug.

"I've never seen a bug like that before. I've never had a reaction like that to any bug bite."

After listening to my answers, they informed me that if I'd had a severe allergic reaction to a bug bite that it would have happened within minutes, or at least the first half hour. It had now been well over an hour. The medics suggested that my body was having a reaction to what the bug had injected in me which had caused me to feel hot, faint, and have trouble breathing. They also mentioned that it was still up to me if I wanted to go to the hospital. The choice was mine.

Next the ambulance showed up with a couple of young medics. They repeated all the questions again, and made suggestions, but still left it up to me. The whole time, I felt very calm, and even mentioned to the young medics how I am basically a calm person who doesn't get hysterical. After *their thorough checking and suggestions, I decided to not go in the ambulance, and off to the hospital. It turned out to be a wise choice, saving me a lot of time, money and hassle. I never got a bill for the visit, but I imagine if they had taken me out on a stretcher to the ambulance that I would have had a very, expensive ride to the hospital.*

Later, I went to bed, struggling to sleep with the still throbbing hand, but I only took an Ibuprofen. Eventually, I fell asleep, but not before wondering what that whole experience meant. The symbolism of the strange bug biting my left hand after I looked at the sign for the Raven's Rest. The call for 911 – a cry for help. The firetruck and the ambulance showing up. My calm presence the whole time while they fussed over me. Was it a cry for help? Was I feeling a need to be taken care of? Maybe the bug bite was some kind of initiation. In any case, I now know what happens when you call 911. If I ever have to call 911 for someone else, I won't hesitate. After all, it's better to be safe than sorry.

After I had that incident with the bug bite, I never told Jim's cousin and her husband who lived at that campground what happened later that night. Once they read this, I hope they'll understand. And that's how I left Oregon with a still, sensitive hand and a new fear of bugs that live in the Northwest.

Chapter 12

National Park Tour

Grand Canyon National Park in Arizona

The goal of many Full-time RVers is to visit the National Parks around the country. It is one of the best bargains that you'll find on the road, and one of the best gifts that you'll ever give yourself. The National Parks are as varied as the states are, and yet, they all capture some unique aspect of the natural beauty of this country. As of 2016, the 100th anniversary of the National Park Service, there were 59 National Parks. Of course, over time, they do add new ones when a National Monument, or another National site gets upgraded to a National Park (NP).

The National Parks pass is definitely worth investing in if you're touring around the country. It's been our favorite pass – giving us access to not only NPs, but federal recreational lands as well.

The entrance fees for the NPs range from free to over $30 each, making the pass a great deal. If you're over 62, you get the best deal of all with a lifetime Golden Age Passport for $10. You can purchase these passes right at the NPs entrance gates. All the details are at www.nationalparks.org (Another benefit of visiting the NPs was finally being able to recycle plastics, aluminum and even cardboard. Most campgrounds only had limited recycling programs or none at all. Hopefully, that will change in the near future.)

Cliff Palace at Mesa Verde National Park in Colorado

Jim and I have been fortunate to visit 36 National Parks as of 2017. Living in the west, we visited several National Parks, and then when we became Full-time RVers, we've seen many more NPs. People always ask us what our favorite parks are, and it really is hard to answer. The most well-known, and usually the largest NPs are in a class of their own – Yellowstone, Yosemite, Grand Canyon, and Hawaii Volcanoes are legendary. They are not to be missed, and seeing them more than once in different seasons is extra special. The National Parks of Alaska, eight altogether, are also incredible, and I hope to make a trip to see them someday.

One of the biggest surprises was the National Parks of Utah. When I began this journey, I had no idea that Utah had five parks. Each Utah NP is remarkable– Arches, Bryce Canyon, Canyonlands, Capitol Reef and Zion, all in the southern portion of Utah. The parks are part of an area known as the Grand Circle, an area in the Southwest with the highest concentration of American scenic parklands in the country. Jim and I were fortunate to see all five Utah parks over several weeks, giving ourselves time to explore each park, and have seen a couple now in different seasons. Jim's favorite is hands down, Bryce Canyon; and mine is Zion, for all the different parts from the towering rock cliffs, to the lush river valley; and the astounding views wherever you walk and hike.

Bryce Canyon National Park in Utah

When we first started Full-time RVing, our goal was to visit National Parks, and other places of natural beauty. We began our NP tour in Florida, and visited the Everglades NP, never realizing how many more parks we would see over these years on the road. When we plan our travel route, we check out what NPs are on the way. If we have to make a detour, we will because the parks are so worth it.

Castle Geyser in Yellowstone National Park

Before visiting a park, I'll read up on the park in one of my guidebooks like the National Geographic's *Guide to the National Parks of the United States* while Jim reads up on-line about that park through the www.nationalparks.org. We then have a general idea of what we want to see in the park along with any hikes. Once we arrive at the entry gate of the park, then we go over the map and brochure that we receive to get a feel for the right hiking trails. If we have time, we always spend at least a couple of days exploring a National Park. For the larger parks, like Yellowstone and Yosemite, we spent a lot more time – six days in Yellowstone with still more to see; and five separate trips to Yosemite in all the different seasons when we lived in California.

For us, it's about savoring the experience – seeing the major sites in the park along with doing a couple of hikes. I've seen people on the news with their selfie sticks, racing around the country to see as many NPs in a year as they can, but they are really missing out on the experience of spending time in nature. It's not so much about doing, but more about being. To see the sunrise over Haleakala Volcano on Maui; to stand at the base of Bridalveil Fall in Yosemite in the springtime; to walk along the rim of the Grand Canyon any time of year; or to hike through the rock formations of Bryce Canyon, gazing up at these miraculous sand castles. These are moments not to be missed, or rushed through. Take your time with the National Parks, and you'll be rewarded with memories that last forever. This adventure is one of my favorite National Park memories.

Travertine Hot Springs in Yellowstone National Park

A National Park Adventure - Blessings of the Bighorns

As I sit writing this story at the kitchen table of my RV, a gale is blowing outside my window. The trees are bending backwards as families of tumbleweeds fly by. I shouldn't be surprised. This week, I am living at Willowwind RV Park in Hurricane, Utah.

When I picked this town for the next stop on my journey around the country, I thought the name was kind of interesting for an inland city in the Southwest. Growing up on Cape Cod, I have seen my share of hurricanes blow their way up the eastern seaboard. But I was pretty confident that Utah hadn't experienced a hurricane except maybe in the distant past when all these startling rock formations were once part of an ancient sea.

View of the Zion Canyon in Zion National Park in Utah

Now, I am thinking they knew what they were doing when they chose this name because the winds on this mid-April *afternoon are gusting close to some of the hurricanes that I have lived through. In my first year on the road, I traveled into the Southwest, and have been following the Grand Circle of scenic parks here. I haven't seen all of them, but last week, I completed the Mighty Five of Utah, the words they use to describe the five national parks in Southern Utah which are Arches, Bryce Canyon, Canyonlands, Capitol Reef and Zion. I began with Zion at the east entrance, and I am now ending my time in Utah at the west and south side of Zion, near Hurricane, Utah.*

West Temple and the Tower of Virgin at Zion National Park in Utah

All five parks have special qualities that are hard to capture in words and pictures. It's the immensity of the parks, and the abundance of rock formations that capture the imagination. Just when you've seen all the rocks you can take in, you'll glimpse another rock, seeming to grow from the desert in a magnificent coat of colors. One of the explorers who mapped this territory called it a "Wilderness of

Rocks."

On my last day of exploring the Mighty Five, I went to Capitol Reef, a national park that I didn't know a lot about. It's a remote park, and not as popular in the guidebooks as Arches or Zion, but since I was here, I wanted to see all that Utah had to offer. After an almost two hour drive, I arrived at the quiet entrance of Capitol Reef. The fee of $5.00 even seemed ridiculous since most movies cost more than that. After getting the map of the park, I headed out for a drive to see the scenic viewpoints. They included more remarkable displays of rock cliffs that stretched for miles off into the horizon. The quieter roads, and peaceful hikes at the viewpoints were a welcome change from the crowds at Arches and Zion. You could have a scenic viewpoint all to yourself.

After a few scenic vistas, I stopped at one of the old farmhouses in the national park which had once been part of a town called Fruita. The small farming community had been established by Mormons, and they had lived an almost utopian way of life here for many years, sustained by an orchard of fruit and nut trees. At the farmhouse, the national park even sold homemade pies which completely won me over to this park.

There was still one more scenic drive to take so off I went to an area called Capitol Gorge. It turns out that I was literally traveling through a wash which is an empty riverbed except when it flashfloods. At the end of the drive, you could then take a hike into this gorge with towering rock walls, inscribed with some petroglyphs from Native Americans, and even the signatures of some of the early pioneers with dates back to the 1800's. The hike in itself was quite memorable, and reading some of the early graffiti was entertaining, but my favorite moment in the park was yet to come.

As I headed back out of the gorge, and back into the wash, the sun dipped lower in the sky. At about quarter to six, I came upon a couple of cars stopped alongside the road. The people were out, all gazing in one direction, and that's when I saw them.

I had been asking for a couple of weeks to see one of these mighty animals in their natural setting. It seemed that they were quite shy, and also not as plentiful as the park would have liked. They had been hunted to almost extinction at one time, and had been introduced back into the park in the 1990's.

As I stepped out of my car, there was the elusive Bighorn sheep, eating the grass near the road. There were three males at different stages of life, all adorned with those astonishing horns. As we all stared at these incredible creatures, they stared back at us not that impressed that they had an audience. They didn't seem threatened by us as long as we all kept our distance. But when two more cars drove up, they sensed too many people, and headed for the rocky cliffs. With a graceful run, they made their way up the cliff with ease. In a matter of minutes, all you could see was the white of their haunches. And now, I knew why I hadn't been able to see them before. They all blended into their rocky hide-out.

Now I am left with the memory of that moment. I was blessed by the three Bighorns. They blessed my own Bighorn RV, and my own journey around the country. I had been calling the Bighorn, the mascot of my journey, and now, I am grateful to have seen them in the wild. I also have a feeling that my Dad had something to do with that special sighting of the Bighorn. He instilled a love of travel in me, and that love continues even though he is no longer with me. Thanks Dad for joining me on my trip of a lifetime.

Big Horn sheep at Capitol Reef National Park in Utah

Chapter 13

Hiking: Our Favorite Pastime

Visiting National Parks, and hiking are our most favorite parts of the Full-time RV journey. Both Jim and I had become avid hikers living in California. We loved going out on the weekends, finding new trails in the Sierra Nevada Mountains, or heading to some of our favorite local parks in the Gold Country such as the South Yuba River State Park, or the Empire Mine State Historic Park, a gold mining museum with some scenic biking and hiking trails. Our hikes were always day hikes though sometimes, we've ended up on some rather long day hikes, lasting 13 hours, not on purpose of course. It's all part of the adventure of exploring new places.

Grand Teton National Park in Wyoming

On our week-end hikes, we had crossed and walked along parts of the Pacific Crest Trail (PCT), but we had never met any PCT hikers up close and personal until this trip around the country. One of my favorite tales is about meeting some PCT hikers on top of the Eastern Sierra Nevada Mountains – I called it from the depths to the heights of my cross-country journey.

In this chapter, I've also included some of our favorite places to hike from traveling around the country. In the Resource section at the end of the book, I also include our list of suggested hiking supplies.

An Adventure from Sea Level to over 10,000 feet

In my travels around the country, I knew I was going to see many different landscapes and seascapes – from the desert to the mountains, from the cozy harbors of the Atlantic to the expansive beaches along the Pacific. But I really didn't think of the depths and heights that I would be exploring in this great country. In this month of May, I have seen Death Valley, the lowest point on the North American continent, and also glimpsed Mt. Whitney, the highest point in the contiguous 48 states. Who knew that they were only about 130 miles from each other?!

In the past month since leaving Utah, I have traveled through Nevada and into Southern and Central California. From the mountains and high desert of the Utah national parks, I have traversed into the lower terrain of this country into the arid desert. Never having lived in the desert for any length of time, the desert has been a new experience for me.

The desert in the spring was likely the most beautiful time to be there. The temperatures were certainly cooler, and the cacti were blooming with their strikingly simple flowers in bright fuchsia and golden yellow. Hiking through washes (riverbeds with no water in them) alongside reddish and golden boulders, I was in another world at times. Some of the desert landscapes resembled the face of the moon, and others looked like a tempting oasis with all the different vegetation.

At first, I enjoyed the desert hikes around Las Vegas, and then into Joshua Tree National Park in Southern California, but then the temperatures rose. The days in the 90's became more common, and the challenges of desert living became more evident. Staying in an RV park near Joshua Tree NP, I saw the number of people in the park dwindle. The RV Park, a winter retreat for many people from the northern states, had a fitness center, indoor pool and spa, and big clubhouse. While I was there, they were almost completely empty. It was time to move north again.

After a week, I traveled north by the Mojave Desert, and onto Highway 395 which is also called the Eastern Sierra Scenic Byway, winding its way through some spectacular scenery with the Eastern Sierra Nevada Mountains on one side, and the Inyo National Forest on the other side. As I left the desert behind and gazed upon the mountains, I could feel the shift in my spirit. The mountains had become my other home when I lived in California all those years. I had driven this same route from the north, but never, all the way to the southern end.

Now, I would finally discover where this incredible highway started in the desert. I had seen the signs for Death Valley

National Park, and I knew I had at least one more desert experience in my near future, but I had no idea what this park encompassed. Driving from the west led to a more diverse experience. As I traveled towards the park, I rode through hills that then turned into mountains. Driving a winding road through the mountains, I dropped lower and lower into the park, and finally the desert valley opened up before me. After the steep descent into Death Valley, there were windswept sand dunes, golden canyons and salt flats that shimmered like mirages. The temperatures skyrocketed. Stopping at one of the visitor centers, there is a permanent large thermometer outside the door, recording the latest temperature. A perfect picture spot. When I was there in mid-May, the temperature fluctuated between 90 to 95 degrees Fahrenheit. I can only imagine what it's like in the summer.

Badwater Basin, Death Valley National Park

Of course, that wasn't the temperature of the lowest point in the park. Driving further down into the park, you arrive at what is called – Badwater Basin, another salt flat with some puddles, but best known as being the lowest elevation on this continent. At 282 feet below sea level, I had reached a new low point, and didn't realize how close it was to the highest point in this country.

Staying in Lone Pine, California right off of Highway 395, I camped in the town closest to the highest point. After exploring the town and visiting their film history museum and the Alabama Hills where many westerns and sci-fi films have been filmed, I decided to explore the highest point in the contiguous forty-eight states – Mount Whitney, a snow-capped peak in the Sierra Nevada Mountains at 14,495 feet.

On a clear morning, it appeared to be a perfect day to drive into the mountain range for a hike. Driving up a road on the outskirts of town, I traveled higher and higher on switchbacks, lined with rocky cliffs, and purple lupine. That's when the clouds drifted across the surrounding peaks. What appeared to be a calm day in the valley turned into a snow squall in the mountains. Snowflakes drifted down onto the windshield of the truck. It looked like I'd have to postpone my mountain hike.

As I crested the peak, the elevation rose to over 10,000 feet and the temperature dropped into the 30s with Mount Whitney hidden by the clouds. I thought about turning back, but not before, looking around this mountain top plateau. And what do I spot under some trees? Not the wildlife I *expected to see, but some weary hikers, loaded with backpacks. A couple of minutes later, they are loaded into the truck for the ride back to town. It turned out that they were hiking the Pacific Crest Trail, and ran into the stormy weather so they needed to take a break to warm up and refuel.*

With my own travel plans in mind, I had forgotten about the many people who venture out each year to tackle the challenge of the Pacific Crest Trail which runs all the way from the Mexican border to the Canadian border, over 2,600 miles. The hikers usually begin in the spring, and hike all summer, and sometimes into the fall. The trail starts in the desert which I had just left behind, and follows the mountain ranges beginning in central California, and then up through the Northwest of Oregon and Washington. I had no idea that I was also following a similar route with my Bighorn RV. Hearing these three hikers' tales was enlightening. It was also a good reminder for all the conveniences that I do live with, traveling in an RV with most of the comforts of home. Even with my love of hiking, I don't think I could take on a challenge like them though I did enjoy hearing about their own adventures. The hikers called us their "PCT Angel" so hopefully, we can help more hikers along the way who need a break from the trail, or a ride back into the mountains. After that meeting, I followed the Pacific Crest Trail more closely as I made my way north, and crossed the trail a few more times in Oregon and Washington. Admiring their courage, I still wonder if those three hikers completed their goal of finishing the PCT all in one year.

Amazing Hiking Adventures

Some of my most incredible hikes took place out in the Wild West in Utah, California and Washington State. As I wrote in Chapter 12, Utah was a big surprise with all those stunning national parks. It's hard to pick a favorite hiking trail. Zion NP had a wide variety of hikes from trails winding up the cliffs with spectacular views of the rocks and the valley below, to scenic paths meandering through the valley over streams, leading to sacred, red rock canyons. The whole time in Zion, I had a front row seat on natural beauty. The following are some of the other places that had unforgettable hikes.

Lundy Canyon in Lee Vining, California

One of my favorite hikes was in the Eastern Sierra Nevada Mountains referred by more than one person who exclaimed how much they relished this hike through Lundy Canyon. Since it was still early May, I expected to see snow on the trails around the Sierra Nevada Mountains, and that did happen at the higher elevations. But the canyon trails didn't have as much snow due to a milder winter. Driving by Lundy Lake, the road twisted and turned into a dirt road flanked by trees on both sides. Finally, Jim and I came to an area with parked cars, and what seemed to be the trail head. Eating lunch sitting on a log overlooking a creek below, we prepared for the hike, stashing power gels and granola bars in our camel backpacks. No one else was around except empty cars so we chose one of the paths. After walking for about ten minutes, it didn't seem to be the right trail. Turning back to the parking area, we walked around some more, and discovered another trail head, thinking this must be the one.

Donna and Jim hiking in Zion National Park

Many times, the great trails don't come with signs pointing you in the right direction. It can take a determined hiker to find them. Being hidden jewels, I think some of the locals want to keep the treasure to themselves. Somehow, we found the right trail. With renewed energy, we hiked through a forest of evergreens and aspens. The trees weren't too tall like there had been a recent fire. The inviting green of the woods inspired me to trek on. Coming out of a grove of trees, I spied Mill Creek where the trail now followed alongside the river, bending and twisting with its turns. For a while, we were still hidden in the woods, but then it opened up, revealing canyon walls on both sides of a valley. I thought, This must be Lundy Canyon.

In this valley, we were treated to an expansive view of the towering walls of the canyon. With the recent rain and snow, rivers poured over the cliffs, spilling into small pools which then splashed into spontaneous waterfalls. Wherever I gazed,

I could see these rushing rivers crashing down the canyon walls. We then climbed up rocky paths that wound their way through the canyon, looking down upon the river below. I could see a beaver's home in the middle of the river with smaller dams of piles of sticks that the beavers had collected.

With the sun overhead, the rivers, the canyon walls, and the trees, Mother Earth embraced me with all four of her elements. The sunshine peeked through the clouds creating the Fire while the Water flowed everywhere in the rivers, and waterfalls pouring down the cliffs. The Earth surrounded me in the rocky cliffs, and the Air whispered in a mountain breeze caressing the evergreen trees. I stood in awe as if I was in an outdoor cathedral. I breathed in all of these elements, and thanked the heavens above for the wonderful blessing of being on this hike.

Lundy Canyon in Lee Vining, California

Jim and I continued on, traveling further into the canyon, wishing the day would never end. As the sun slipped behind the canyon walls, we sat at the base of one of the waterfalls that had made its way to the floor of the canyon. Two other hikers came around the corner further along the path, waving as they headed home. It was time to turn around, and yet hard to leave all this splendor behind. Walking back and savoring my steps, I knew this hike would stay with me longer than today. And it has. The memory of that explosion of spring in the Eastern Sierra Nevada Mountains won't ever be forgotten.

Skyline Trail in Mount Rainier National Park in Washington State

Having visited Washington a few years ago, Jim and I had been to the Olympic NP on the coast, delighting in a mountain ridge hike, but we had missed the inland Mount Rainier NP. Driving from our campground in Silver Creek, Washington, we headed to Mount Rainier NP, anticipating more evergreen forests, and historical sights, but not expecting to be blown away by another spectacular hike.

Winding our way up to the Henry Jackson Visitors Center, we ventured outside to discover the trail head for the Skyline Trail. Looming above us, the peak of Mount Rainier at 14,410 feet, the highest mountain in the Cascade Mountain range, was shrouded in a ring of clouds. At first, the trail descended down, leading us towards the Myrtle Falls. We strolled by fields of wildflowers, admiring a summer day in the mountains. Gazing down at the falls, we contemplated going any further. It was mid-afternoon on a brilliant blue sky day with hours of daylight to go. I am so glad that we decided to continue the climb.

Skyline Trail in Mount Rainier National Park

As we hiked higher and higher, the flowers grew more in abundance, and flowed down the hillsides in a rainbow of colors from the purple lupine to the magenta and scarlet paint brushes, from the pink monkeyflowers to the white lilies. With the high peaks above us still covered with the remnants of ancient glaciers, we were greeted with green vistas of fields and evergreens wherever we looked. The Tatoosh Mountain range glowed in the distance like a ribbon of fairy tale castles. Its rocky pinnacles didn't seem real like a mirage of mountains.

Along the path, animals and birds greeted us. Stellar jays with their brilliant blue feathers and distinct voices swooped down from tree to tree. A solitary eagle circled over the cloud-covered peaks. A young doe ate her late afternoon lunch by the side of the trail. Furry marmots meandered through the fields of flowers, munching off the tops of flowers with a relish for their colorful salad.

At the height of summer in the mountains, rivers sprung from the slopes, and wound their way down through brilliantly colored mosses of green and gold. Wherever you looked, you could see rivers circling into pools of water, and then spilling over edges into waterfalls. In the distance, rain poured down on a hillside, and in the midst of a sun break, a rainbow broke through the clouds, spanning across the green hills. It made me wonder if there wasn't truly a pot of gold beneath its colorful ribbons. On our drive back down leaving the Skyline Trail behind, I looked up, and through the clouds, Mount Rainier showed her weather-beaten face. It was the perfect ending to a day spent honoring that mountain.

Every time, I turned a corner on the Skyline Trail I wondered what miracle I was going to see next. It was one of the most magical hikes I've ever been on. Since it was a Sunday afternoon, there were quite a few families out on the trail, and groups of college students. All different nationalities and cultures walked along the trail. And everyone greeted each other with similar amazement at all the natural beauty that surrounded us. It made me hopeful that the national parks could have a higher purpose of bringing people together from diverse backgrounds in coexistence with a mutual love of nature. It could certainly be a starting point for Peace. If we could all stop and really see this planet Earth that we call home, knowing that it's up to each one of us to take care of our planet, and in doing so, we would be taking care of all living beings including humankind. As John Lennon once sang, "Imagine."

Chapter 14

Pacific Coast Adventures

Growing up on Cape Cod, I've had a love affair with the ocean a long time. At times, I have lived away from the coast, but I always had a longing to be back by the sea. Even now, after traversing across this great country, I still find it hard to imagine living in the middle so far from both the Atlantic and the Pacific Oceans. Some of my most memorable moments have taken place near the ocean. These tales are from my time on the Northwest coast which I would highly recommend spending at least three months there because of all the sights to see. Jim and I were there from June through August in one year, and could have spent even another month or two with all the national and state parks in those states. Here are some of my favorite places.

Redwoods National Park, Crescent City, California

Ever since, I first saw the Redwoods in the Muir Woods near San Francisco, I have been in awe of these towering beauties. In their presence, I feel like I have stepped into a sacred temple, encircled by the wisdom of these ancient trees. Even though, they are not the oldest trees in the world (the Bristlecone pines are the oldest), they are certainly one of the tallest trees, looming overhead like natural skyscrapers.

Redwoods National Park in California

I can still remember reading about the young woman, Julia Butterfly Hill, who took a stand to save the Redwoods, by literally camping high up in one of her precious trees which she named Luna. Up in this 180 foot tall tree known to be about 1500 years old, Julia stayed there for 738 days, keeping the local logging company from cutting it down. In recent years, the state of California and the Save-the-Redwoods League have made some headway with limiting the logging of these majestic giants by acquiring groves of trees and protecting them within over 20 state and national parks. One of these natural sanctuaries is the Redwoods National Park.

When I lived in California, I had only traveled as far north in that state as the city of Eureka where I drove through the Redwoods State Park, drinking in the beauty of those trees that lined the coasts. I had longed to go further, and see the Redwoods NP. The Redwoods NP is at the northern edge of the coastal Redwoods that once covered two million acres. As Jim and I traveled the length of the state, we decided that this was our chance to finally visit the national park. We actually left our RV in the Emigrant RV Park near Ashland, Oregon, and drove through the mountains back into California. The drive alone was glorious through the evergreens, and eventually to the Redwoods.

Dipping back into California, I glimpsed the best of the natural beauty of that state, the Redwoods, and the Pacific Ocean. Being a week-day in June, the Redwoods NP was as quiet and still as the trees that the park honored. Walking along the paths carpeted with pine needles, we sauntered up and down gentle hills with ferns bursting in their early summer colors of golden greens. As the path dove deeper into the forest, we strolled by groves of old growth Redwoods that hadn't been logged in many years. In circles of three or more trees, the Redwoods appeared to be meeting in a holy ceremony of their own creation. I stepped into the middle of one of these circles, and breathed in some of the highest energy that I've felt out in nature. I experienced the "green" energy that James Redfield of The Celestine Prophecy made known in his books. So uplifting, healing and pure, the energy of these natural giants. I imagined what it would be like to live in the energy of the Redwoods all the time, being so close to the mountains and the ocean. Could this be one of the highest energetic points on the planet with the meeting of all three of these energies coming together? It would certainly rival many other natural wonders around the globe.

I found it hard to leave the California Redwoods behind, knowing it would be a while before I walked among them again. Jim and I continued our short drive to the coastal town of Crescent City, California. Like Eureka, this seacoast village reminded me of the small towns in New England that line the Atlantic Ocean. With piers jutting out into the sea, there were fishing boats tied up while fishermen in their waders worked the shore with nets, scooping up their catch. Seagulls joined in the action, swooping down to catch fish that slipped out of the nets. A brisk breeze blew off the water. A fog bank rested off the coast, waiting to crawl in as the sun grew lower in the sky. A mermaid statue posed on one of the piers. I climbed up into her lap for a silly postcard picture.

Sitting at a bench by the sea, I lingered, not wanting to leave California or the ocean behind. I knew I would see the seacoast again in Oregon, but not sure when I would be back in California. After living there for 17 years, it had become home to me – my west coast home. As the sun sunk lower, Jim and I turned back towards the evergreens and the mountains, winding our way back to Oregon with another everlasting experience for the memory book.

A Newport on the West Coast

Newport, Rhode Island on the east coast is one of my favorite towns, but I had never visited a Newport on the west coast even while living in California. Leaving Ashland on Jim's birthday, we drove to Newport, Oregon where we'd celebrate his June birthday that night.

As we drove through the hills of evergreens, we meandered alongside rivers and fields of flowing grass. I anticipated seeing the Oregon coast, knowing how different it would be from my own hometown on Cape Cod. When we turned onto U.S. Route 101, we drove right alongside the ocean. Peeking through the evergreens, I spotted the rocky coastline of Oregon, and the dramatic cliffs going down to the beaches below. At first peek, it certainly didn't look like California, and yet, it did remind me of a few different places. The Oregon coastline was a blending of the sand dune beaches of Cape Cod with the dramatic California coastline, and the rocky outcroppings of the Maine coast. I loved the combination.

Yaquina Head Lighthouse in Newport, Oregon

Driving into Newport, an authentic seaport, with fishing boats gliding into the harbor, we crossed one last steep, stone bridge into town. Our campground was tucked under that bridge with a view of the seacoast all around. Since it was

Jim's birthday, we had to go out and celebrate. There was a local brewery right near the campground – perfect for a casual dinner. Walking by the towering, stainless steel containers, we hiked up some worn, wooden steps for a window-side table alongside the bar. Sampling some of the local brews along with the seafood, I toasted Jim on his Newport birthday, wishing him a new beginning on the horizon. (In that moment, I wondered where I would be for my September birthday. Celebrating in Newport, Rhode Island was an option, and that's what we did later that year.)

With the sun setting behind the bridge, the fog swooped in, and threw a cover right over the bridge's stone arch. Glad I had brought along a fleece jacket, the temperature dropped to a chilly damp 50 degrees. Walking back to my campsite, this was certainly a different beach experience from my days on Cape Cod. During the rest of our time on the Oregon coast, I experienced the brisk days at the beach even when the sun did shine. The beaches stretched for miles, only interrupted by rocky points, and lighthouses that dotted the coast. Visiting one lighthouse, I walked along a path through flowering bushes, and started to really sneeze. The sea coast flowers blooming in July must have been like the spring flowers that caused me to sneeze on the east coast. I recognized similar coastal flowers like hydrangeas in brilliant purples and blues, reminding me of the bushes on Cape Cod.

Spending time in Newport was a coastal treat. With the sea breezes and the bracing nights, it was hard to imagine that on the other side of the inland mountain range, a heat wave had descended. Breathing in all the high energy from the evergreens and the Pacific Ocean, I wished I could take some of that cool, coastal weather with me in my backpack for later.

Friday Harbor on San Juan Island in Washington State

Friday Harbor

Camping near Burlington, Washington, I longed to see the San Juan Islands. Several California friends had raved about these islands, and their rustic beauty. North of Seattle, in the Puget Sound, these islands are sprinkled across the sea like emerald jewels. On a Friday morning, Jim and I chose to take the ferry to Friday Harbor, one of the more popular towns on San Juan Island. We tried to make ferry reservations, but the ticket office had computer glitches that day so they encouraged us to drive down to the pier. As we neared the coastline, we spotted the signs for the island ferries, beginning to look for a parking space for our rather large truck.

On a Friday morning in July, the lots were already filling up.

We tried one parking lot, then another, and yet another. With time slipping away to get to the ferry, I grew anxious. Finally, we found a parking lot atop a hill, but then we had to walk all the way down to the ferry. Getting later and later with each minute, we alternated between walking and running all the way down to the ferry station. The whole time, I'm thinking that we'll have to take a later ferry.

More familiar with airplane travel, I would never think of showing up to catch a plane five minutes before the flight. And yet, that is exactly what we did that Friday morning in Washington. We literally bought our ticket, and walked onto the ferry with barely a minute to spare. It certainly made for a short wait on the boat. With a brisk wind blowing off the water, we stood on the bow of the ship as long as we could, taking in the view of the Puget Sound.

A sunny clear sky day greeted us as we drifted into the port of Friday Harbor. It was first love with this quaint town atop the hill. Walking around the narrow streets of shops and restaurants, Jim and I found a perfect spot for lunch, sitting outside with a view of the downtown, and the dock where the ferries came in. Looking at our options for a day visit, we decided to take the local bus around the island. The bus stopped at all the favorite sights including a lavender farm with a festival going on this week-end, and a lighthouse on the other side of the island where you could sometimes spot whales swimming by. Both sounded delightful, but after seeing the lavender farm from a distance, I chose the Lime

Kiln Lighthouse.

The states of Oregon and Washington treasure their old lighthouses, reminding me of New Englanders and their love of their lighthouses. As the bus dropped us off, a tiny museum and shop attracted our attention where they gave a brief history of the lighthouse. We then strolled along a path to the waterfront, and a close-up view of the Lime Kiln Lighthouse. Walking right alongside the rocky beach, we gazed off towards Vancouver and Canada in the distance. Hoping to see whales spouting in the sea, we only glimpsed sea birds swooping down into the water. The lighthouse was a beauty. With blue sky and smooth seas, its shining beacon wasn't needed by passing ships that day. Sitting on a bench, we overheard conversations in a few different languages, realizing that the San Juan Islands appealed to many people, even those from around the world.

Eventually, we had to head back to the port of Friday Harbor. I inquired of the local bus driver, an elderly lady who obviously relished her summer job, about the year-round weather. She said, "In the summer, a warm day is in the 70s, and once and a while, we hit 90, but the winters are a lot cooler and wetter. It's not weather for everyone, but those who live here, love it."

I believe it's the dream of the island life. It's a fantasy for many people to live on an island, but the reality of island life is that it doesn't suit everyone. There are the quiet seasons of winter when you need to entertain yourself more. I would imagine that's why you find many artists and writers living on islands. They prefer the solitude, and the time to create on their own. I've always been fascinated by living on an island especially a tropical island chain like the Hawaiian islands, but I also know that I would probably miss jumping on a highway, and driving for miles to another state, and a new place. Not something you can do as easily when you live on an island.

My time with the San Juan Islands was short, but sweet. I definitely experienced their appeal. As Jim and I sat at another outdoor table, sampling some cheese and crackers while sipping chardonnay, I could feel the pull of the island, and wished that my time there didn't have to end. But it was time to get back on the ferry, heading towards the mainland and more adventures.

Chapter 15

Exit Strategy

In our three years of traveling around the country, we've met many Full-timers from newbies to RVers who've been on the road from five to eight years, and even longer. One couple had been Full-timers for 10 years, and then bought a house in a place that they always loved to visit. Now, they travel six months of the year, becoming one of those part-time Full-timers.

No matter what age you are when you begin the Full-time lifestyle, you may want to have a plan for the future when living on the road Full-time isn't your dream life anymore. It doesn't have to be a plan written in stone because maybe, you are on this journey to find that next place to call home. You may want to think about what your options are for the future. In this chapter, I'm going to cover some of those options.

One option for the future is buying a house or a condominium in one of your favorite places to visit which is probably the easiest to imagine especially if you've just left your home behind. You may still have some of your belongings in storage, and even planned on setting up a home again someday. There are all kinds of reasons to establish a traditional home again from wanting to live near family and friends, to having a community around you in one location; and from needing more living space, to having a yard again because you love to garden.

At some point, you may also want to be near your circle of support again including your doctor, dentist, hairdresser, etc. Many RVers seem to make this decision as they get older, and need to be closer to doctors and people that they depend on. If you have family and friends in more than one area, and you're open to working with a new support team, then you may be open to other options.

Staying in so many different campgrounds the first year of our travels, Jim and I saw many people who were living in one campground Full-time. Like us, they had sold their traditional home, and downsized into an RV, but they were content with keeping their RV home in one campground. Sometimes, it was a financial decision because they still worked in the area, or moved there for a job. Other times, they had moved to the area that they loved, and wanted to call home, but we're not quite ready to give up the RV lifestyle. It certainly is a great way to try living in different areas of the country, and get to know the surrounding towns, and even the neighborhoods before you decide to buy a traditional home there.

Some RVers also have two locations that they go back and forth between: One campground for the winter/spring, and one for the summer/fall. That's also another option, and probably the best of both worlds. If you live in a colder climate, then you may love to head south for the winter. An RV home makes it very affordable to live in two different places – a lot less expensive than having to buy two homes.

In the second and third year of our travels, Jim and I have been staying in campgrounds longer especially since Jim started doing workamping stints. We've lived in Florida for five months, in Utah for four months, and then North Carolina for another four months. It really gave us the opportunity to explore a new area, and imagine ourselves living there. Staying in one place longer, we also met people who had moved there, and were living in the campground Full-time. It gave us a chance to meet some of the "locals" and find out what it's really like to live there longer than a season. This method also seemed to be a good way to try out different regions of the country, and decide on a future location for a traditional home.

One of the biggest reasons that people give up the Full-time RV life is when they are no longer able to do it physically. Some make that decision before their health becomes an issue, but most start to notice the signs, and then look at their options. One of the best options for those who want to continue to live in their RV is the Escapees CARE (Continuing Assistance for Retired Escapees) program www.escapeescare.org which is a nonprofit adult day care and residency program designed for RVers who are unable to travel for a time because of age, injury, sickness or surgery. The facility is located next to the Escapees Rainbow's End campground in Livingston, Texas. They have set aside a certain amount of RV sites for Escapees independent living along with some sites for volunteers who assist with the program.

The Escapees CARE, Inc. is governed by a volunteer Board of Directors, with a professional staff running the facility. The requirements are that you be an Escapees member, and able to pay one month in advance. Because the facility is non-profit, they receive donations, and volunteer support which allows them to offer their services at a lower cost. Many people stay there for only a short time to deal with a health issue requiring surgery, or stay longer depending on their health situation. For a Full-time RVer, it's an ideal situation to be able to receive health care and support while still living in your RV home. The program is quite popular with a waiting list, and possible future plans of expansion with similar facilities in new areas. With the Baby Boomer population retiring, and more people joining the ranks of Full-timers, it seems that the Escapees CARE program could continue to grow and expand in the future. It is certainly a worthwhile nonprofit to support especially if you see yourself using their services down the road someday.

Our own exit strategy recently materialized. Both my husband and I didn't have a clear plan about what we would do after Full-timing. We came to the Full-time RV lifestyle when everything seemed to be ending, and leading us in a new direction. Since the direction wasn't clear, we decided to give the RV lifestyle a try. We hadn't been dreaming about RVing in retirement, but it seemed to be a good option to see the country while we could. It also allowed us time to explore what we'd like to do next in our lives, and where we would like to live. Honestly, I thought we'd be out on the road for only a year, and then it lead to a second year, and now a third year. I think that's how it works out here on the road. It's a timeless life because you're living a non-mainstream kind of life. You're not following the traditional lifestyle so time does seem to expand when you're not rushing through your life to get to the next week-end. You live more in the moment.

After our three years on the road, I longed to have one home that stayed in one place. My husband and I built our first home, 30 years ago, and now, we're going to build what could be our last home in our original home state of Massachusetts. After living away for 20 years, we'll both be close to the hometowns where we grew up years ago. Some people say you can't go home again, but we're going to give it a try. We'll still keep our Bighorn RV, and spend winter/spring in warmer locations so we'll join the ranks of the part-time Full-Timers. It will be the best of both worlds. We'll soon be starting another chapter in our lives. In the meantime, we'll see you out on the open road, and look forward to hearing from you about your RVing travels. Best of luck on Living the RV Lifestyle.

The Final Adventure – Saltwater in my Blood

As I traveled towards the middle of the country, I followed the highway in my Rand McNally Road Atlas, loving the big picture view of my trip. When I folded open the page to the map of the whole country, the town of Junction City, Kansas was literally in the fold of the map. Back in 2014, we traveled there to check out an RV that was on Jim's wish list.

Entering Kansas, Jim and I drove on a meandering road that went up and down over small hills with cornfields unraveling off into the distance. We were visiting New Horizons, a specialty RV manufacturer that only made custom mobile homes. The company was near Junction City, Kansas. After our tour of the plant and checking out a couple of used mobile homes, we went out to dinner in town. It was a college town so there were several restaurants and bars, more than I would have expected. But the whole time I was there, smack in the middle of the country, I had a claustrophobic feeling that the ocean was too far away. I haven't always lived near the ocean, but in the Gold Country of California, I could get to the San Francisco Bay in a couple of hours.

Staying in the middle of the country made me realize that I really need to be closer to the ocean. When you've grown up in a place like Cape Cod, it's hard to live without all those bays and beaches that line the New England coast. Away from the ocean, I always did feel like a fish out of water which makes sense with a name like Fisher.

My Father, Donald Fisher, grew up literally on the water with the high tide washing up under his house in Spile City in Onset, Massachusetts. This ramshackle collection of homes was named for the piers that supported the homes over the water alongside Broad Cove, leading to Dummy Bridge. Another curious name which described the dummy cars that once ran along that bridge.

The seacoast village of Onset is part of Wareham which is considered the Gateway to Cape Cod. Later, I found an old magazine called, The Compass which wrote about a stone marker that had been placed in 1739 on the border of West Wareham and Rochester, MA. This stone rock engraved with the words, Cape Cod, marked the true beginning of Cape Cod where the soil turned sandy, and the scrub pine trees popped up, replacing the taller pines. Of course, this marker was placed long before the Cape Cod Canal which was a man-made division for the Cape, and obviously not the original beginning of Cape Cod. I found the marker for myself along Mary's Pond Road, and felt like an explorer uncovering the truth.

My Mother, Doris Fisher, also came from Cape Cod, having grown up in West Wareham and Rochester as a young girl. Her childhood home literally sat on the border of the two towns, where you could cross the street and be in Rochester, or cross back, and be in West Wareham. Even though she had grown up that close to the ocean, she hadn't spent a lot of time at the beach. Her parents both had to work to make a *living, and my Mom was left in charge of her siblings to make sure they did housework as well as homework.* Her childhood wasn't a carefree time at the beach like my Dad who called his childhood in Onset like "living in one big playground." His life wasn't idyllic either, having lost his Mom when he was not even two, and losing his own Dad in a sense as he wasn't around a lot. Lucky for my Dad, his grandparents raised him well even if they did give him a great deal of freedom as a boy. My Dad, shared that love of the outdoors and the ocean with his three daughters. And truth be told, I do believe I inherited saltwater in my blood.

View from our land on Cape Cod, Massachusetts

That's why, I couldn't be happier to be buying this land on Cape Cod, Massachusetts. Living near the ocean once again is going to be like heaven for me. It's time to go Home.

About the Photographer

J. Alan "Jim" Jackson has many hobbies but among them, photography was one of his first passions. Before Jim was a teenager he received a fully manual 35mm SLR camera from his Grandfather. He experimented first with black & white film and learned to develop that film in his Grandfather's basement lab. From that day forward he was hooked. Jim was "that person" who always had his camera at the ready to take pictures at events. From college gatherings to family parties, and well, just about anything. So then with his love of the outdoors, Jim had the perfect venue to continue to develop his keen eye for finding that unique lighting or beautiful vista and, of course, documenting the journey. Jim has a Bachelor of Science in Mechanical Engineering from Northeastern University. But among his hobbies of woodworking, Jack-of-All-Trades, handyman skills, computers/software and web development/marketing, Jim's first passion remains photography.

About the Author

Originally from Cape Cod, Massachusetts, Donna Fisher-Jackson most recently lived in Northern California in the San Francisco Bay area for 7 years, and in the Gold Country of the Sierra Nevada foothills for 10 years. In 2014, Donna, and her husband, Jim, with their cat, Zeus sold most of their belongings, and began a whole new lifestyle as Full-time RVers. Donna always had a love of travel, visiting many countries around the world, but this has been her first journey completely in the United States with a brief visit to Canada.

Donna also continues her work in the counseling field on the road. Her counseling business is Iris Holistic Counseling Services which she began in 1999. With her clients, she shares the insights of Hypnotherapy, the Enneagram, Past-Life Regression, Western Astrology and the Mythic Tarot.

She has an M.A. in Counseling Psychology specializing in Holistic Studies from John F. Kennedy University of Northern California. She has also written the non-fiction book, *The Healing Path of the Romantic* on the Type Four of the Enneagram Personality Type System.

A Certified Hypnotherapist, Donna utilizes past-life regression in her counseling business as a healing tool. Based on her own past life memories, she wrote the novel, *Clara & Irving: A Love Story of Past Lives* which takes place in the 1920's and the present time with many scenes at the Zeiterion Theatre, a performing arts center in New Bedford, MA where she once worked as the Director of Public Relations.

Donna looks forward to continuing her RV travels for many years even while living in her next dream home on Cape Cod. As Ralph Waldo Emerson once said, "Life is a journey, not a destination."

Resource section

Suggested Important Papers for Life on the Road

- ☐ Passports
- ☐ Copy of your will
- ☐ Titles for your vehicles
- ☐ Social Security cards
- ☐ Copies of Birth and Marriage certificates
- ☐ Financial documents – Tax returns for three years, and Investment records
- ☐ Vehicle Insurance documents
- ☐ Health Insurance information including your personal health records
- ☐ Real estate documents for any property owned
- ☐ Contracts for Cell phones, Satellite television, Workamper agreements, etc.

(Of course, some of these documents can be stored on your computer, and on back-up drives. We kept one back-up drive in the RV, and one in our second vehicle. We also left a fireproof safe with all of our important documents at a family member's home.)

Jim's Essential and Suggested Gear for the RV Lifestyle

Essential Tools and Supplies:

- ☐ Tire pressure gauge – use it all the time.
- ☐ Portable air compressor to inflate low tires - If you don't have a generator, make sure you get a good 12VDC compressor.
- ☐ Torque wrench to check the lug nuts torque
- ☐ Volt meter to check continuity and voltages
- ☐ Duct tape 1,001 uses
- ☐ Roadside hazard reflectors and flares
- ☐ Pair of high quality rubber gloves for handling the sewer pipes
- ☐ All-purpose tool kit, screw drivers, plyers, wrenches, sockets, cutters, knife, hammer, pry bar, drill bits, etc.
- ☐ Good flashlights
- ☐ Jumper cables
- ☐ Spare brake fluid, oil, antifreeze, windshield washer fluid
- ☐ Extra fire extinguisher
- ☐ Roof repair kit
- ☐ Spare light bulbs
- ☐ GPS made for RVers
- ☐ Assorted nuts, bolts, washers, screws, nails, hose clamps, tie wraps, wire connectors, wire, electrical tape, and permanent marker

- ☐ Portable drill/driver
- ☐ Standard extension cord, 25 foot
- ☐ 30A/50A socket adaptor
- ☐ Water supply filter
- ☐ Water Pressure reducer set to 40PSI. Use it all the time! You never know what pressure you will encounter in RV parks.
- ☐ Road atlas
- ☐ Wheel chocks and leveling pads or Anderson camper levers

Suggested Gear:

- ☐ Tow strap, just in case
- ☐ Tire pressure monitoring system - Could save a lot of money in RV repairs if you can stop before the tire fails and destroys your undercarriage.
- ☐ Spare fuel tank(s)
- ☐ Sturdy gloves
- ☐ Surge protector for the whole RV. It saved us once!
- ☐ Tie down straps
- ☐ 25 foot RV extension cord
- ☐ Tarp
- ☐ Heated fresh water hose for cold conditions
- ☐ Spare 25 foot drinking water hose(s)
- ☐ Step ladder, 6 foot and a small step stool
- ☐ Knee pads

- ☐ Inline water meter so you know how much water you're putting into your tank.
- ☐ Reverse RV flush valve. Let's you clean your tanks plus if you have a leaky valve, it keeps you from making a mess when hooking up your sewer hose.
- ☐ King pin stabilizer for 5th Wheel RVs

Suggested Hiking Supplies for Day Hikes

- ☐ Hiking boots/walking shoes
- ☐ Telescoping hiking stick, or you can always find a stick on the trail.
- ☐ Fleece jacket/warm coat with gloves & hat for cooler mountain hikes
- ☐ Light windbreaker with hood for possible rain & very, misty waterfalls
- ☐ Deet mosquito repellant
- ☐ GPS- less chance of getting lost in the mountains
- ☐ Fanny pack for shorter hikes
- ☐ Backpack/Camelback for longer hikes
- ☐ Hat for sun/rain protection
- ☐ Extra socks
- ☐ Small Camelback and/or water bottles
- ☐ Water purification tablets or a siphon
- ☐ Waterproof matches
- ☐ Hand sanitizer- Travel size
- ☐ Sun tan lotion – Travel size

- ☐ Power gels & Energy bars
- ☐ Sunglasses
- ☐ Small first aid kit
- ☐ Bear spray if needed
- ☐ Bear bell
- ☐ Emergency Survival blanket (folded up into a small square)
- ☐ Whistle and thermometer tied to backpack
- ☐ Small binoculars
- ☐ All-purpose knife
- ☐ Parachute cord
- ☐ Flashlight
- ☐ Compass
- ☐ Leave a note in your RV where you went hiking, and when you expect to return; and also in your car at the trail head.

Opening and Closing the Fifth Wheel RV Check Lists

These lists were created for our particular needs, and will not apply to all situations.

DO NOT GET DISTRACTED WHILE PERFORMING THESE TASKS!

Fifth Wheel – Closing Check List - Inside

- ☐ Lower TV antenna
- ☐ Secure TVs
- ☐ Lower window blinds
- ☐ Close vents
- ☐ Secure all chairs, kitchen table, recliners, cabinet doors, shower doors, sliding doors to bathroom and front closet
- ☐ Lower stove cover
- ☐ Lay towels over bottom shower door track (prevents water from coming out on floor)
- ☐ Shut off water heater
- ☐ Water pump off
- ☐ Fireplace off
- ☐ Secure kitchen faucet handle with bungee cord
- ☐ Secure fridge door and items inside
- ☐ Remove all items from counters, bureau, vanity and desk
- ☐ Secure lamp
- ☐ Re-check that all items are secure
- ☐ Close all slide-outs
- ☐ Kitchen - make sure racks are locked in place

- [ ] Large kitchen cabinet - place pin in sliding section
- [ ] Retract awning
- [ ] Secure outside steps

Closing and Hitching Fifth Wheel to Truck List

- [ ] Do not remove wheel chocks until ready to travel
- [ ] Raise rear stabilizer jacks
- [ ] Dump waste water as needed (add chemicals to black water tank)
- [ ] Fill fresh water tank if not going to a full hookup campground for 1 or 2 days
- [ ] Disconnect TV cable
- [ ] Disconnect electrical lines
- [ ] Disconnect water and remove pressure gauge
- [ ] Raise steps to trailer and secure safety handrail
- [ ] Raise trailer to clear tailgate
- [ ] Back truck to hitch (make sure trailer pin clears tailgate)
- [ ] Make sure trailer rides up on hitch preventing high pinning and locks (using flashlight make sure trailer pin is locked in hitch)
- [ ] Secure breakaway wire and place lock on hitch handle
- [ ] Plug in trailer wiring to truck
- [ ] Remove wheel chocks
- [ ] Lock all trailer doors
- [ ] Make one complete walk around trailer

- ☐ If tight campsite have someone observe that you are clearing all obstacles
- ☐ Check air ride level (Add air only when hitched to truck)

Fifth Wheel – Opening/Set-up Check List

- ☐ When parking check that all slide-outs can open freely (trees, picnic table or post)
- ☐ Add wheel blocks to level as needed
- ☐ Chock wheels on each side of trailer
- ☐ Lower front legs to take weight off truck
- ☐ Disconnect trailer wiring and breakaway cable from truck
- ☐ Pull pin on hitch in truck bed
- ☐ Slowly pull truck out from under trailer (stop and check that trailer pin will clear tailgate)
- ☐ Raise trailer as needed to clear tailgate
- ☐ Level trailer front to rear (using front level)
- ☐ Lower rear stabilizer jacks
- ☐ Connect water hose with pressure valve
- ☐ Connect electrical cord
- ☐ Open slide-outs (check that no cabinet doors opened during travel)
- ☐ Fill water system (before turning hot water heater on) could burn out heater if dry.
- ☐ Open hot & cold faucet to bleed air from water system
- ☐ Check that fridge is operating in correct mode & temp.

- ☐ Start water heater (If the system has been turned off, and you're using propane to heat the water, then you will need to light burner on stove to bleed air from line.)
- ☐ Extend awning
- ☐ Remove straps from recliners, dinette and TVs.
- ☐ Connect cable or raise antenna (Use antenna reminder)
- ☐ Connect sewer hose

Handy Apps

- GasBuddy – Find cheap gas near you.
- RVparky – Find RV parks with reviews, and you can put your settings in the app.
- Allstays – Find RV parks with reviews, and can put your settings in the app.
- Waze – A community-based traffic and navigation app where drivers in your area share real-time traffic and road information.
- Rest stops – Find rest stops on your highway route.
- Satellite director - Find the satellite so you know what direction to point your dish.
- RVillage – Connect with other RVers wherever you are in an RV park.
- Google Maps/ Google Earth

Helpful websites

- ☐ www.RV-Dreams.com - A great website chock full of RVing information posted by Howard and Linda Payne who've been Full-time RVers since age 41, and on the road since 2005. They host RV rallies that introduce newbies to the RV lifestyle, and you don't even need an RV to attend. A great way to learn about the Full-time RV lifestyle.
- ☐ www.RVReviews.net - Reviews of all kinds of Recreational vehicles.
- ☐ www.pods.com - Storage containers that make moving a lot easier.
- ☐ www.escapees.com – The Escapees RV Club is a great help with rallies, campgrounds, educational programs, mail forwarding and is worth looking into for all the benefits.
- ☐ www.escapeescare.org - Escapees CARE (Continuing Assistance for Retired Escapees) program which is located at the Rainbow's End Escapees Campground in Livingston, Texas.
- ☐ www.goodsamclub.com - Good Sam's is another worthwhile RV Club to explore with discounts at campgrounds, gas stations, along with their Roadside Assistance and Travel Assist programs.
- ☐ www.RVParkReviews.com – A good site for finding campground reviews around the country.
- ☐ www.RV-camping.org - All kinds of camping options from private to public campgrounds, from boondocking to free

camping. The site is also a great resource for articles, and tips on the RV lifestyle.

- ☐ www.reserveamerica.com - Handles reservations for several state park systems as well as federal campgrounds.
- ☐ www.blm.gov/wo/st/en.html Bureau of Land Management, the place to go to find those public lands where you can do some boondocking/dry camping.
- ☐ www.freecampgrounds.com – This website provides advice and ideas on where to find free and cheap camping.
- ☐ www.casinocamper.com - A great resource for casinos that allow camping for free or at a low cost.
- ☐ www.workamper.com - One of the main resources for finding jobs while living the RV lifestyle.
- ☐ www.coolworks.com - Another good source for jobs around the country.
- ☐ www.nationalparks.org – The best entertainment deal around the country.

Made in the USA
San Bernardino, CA
06 June 2017